SmiLeage

SmiLeage

Fun travel games
&
activities for all ages

Michael Nolan

Cumberland House
Nashville, Tennessee

Published by Cumberland House Publishing, Inc., 231 Harding Industrial Drive, Nashville, Tennessee 37211.

Jacket design by Will Owen.
Interior design by Brenda Pope.

Library of Congress Cataloging-in-Publication Data

Nolan, Mike, 1957-
     Smileage : fun travel games & activities for all ages / Michael Nolan.
          p. cm.
     ISBN 1-888952-43-1 (paper : alk. paper)
     1. Games for travelers. I Title.
   GV1206.N65 1997
   794—dc21   97-6312
                                                                        CIP

Printed in the United States of America
2 3 4 5 6 7—02 03 01 00 99 98

To Nancy

my traveling companion for life

Contents

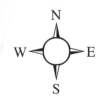

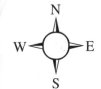

Acknowledgments

Thanks to my parents, Joe and Mildred Nolan, who believed in the value of vacations; several hundred fellow travelers through the years, especially the multiple generations of senior high students at Belmont Church; Bernie Sheahan and the sojourners of the Blue Highways Tours; the Dudes, who offer relentless support and encouragement; agent extraordinaire Sara Fortenberry; and everyone who took the time to offer their ideas on making the miles fly.

Introduction

"How long till we get there?"

It's the most dreaded question of whoever is in charge of a long trip. We tend to think in terms of destinations, forgetting what songwriter Michael Card describes as "a joy in the journey."

This book is intended for any group that's going places—the family en route to Grandma's house, the friends headed to the mountains, the youth group headed for a retreat, the marching band bound for the Macy's Thanksgiving Day parade, the college students breaking for the beach, and senior citizens on the charter bus set on spending their children's inheritance.

As a road warrior myself, I've had ample reason to find ways to make the miles go by more enjoyably. I've learned that having a good time as you go can make even a long, barren ribbon of free-way seem a rather fine place to be.

Many of my favorite conversations have taken place at 2 A.M. when we highway-hypnotized sojourners struggled to keep each other awake. In those unguarded moments we were just too tired to keep our defenses up, and stronger bonds of friendship were forged. I wouldn't trade those times for the world.

Making the Most of This Book

Sure, you can use this book to swat flies, scrape crumbs off the seat, or fan yourself when the air conditioner loses its cool, but I actually had higher hopes.

I was thinking maybe you might use your time to sharpen your wit, test your memory, think creatively, play a game or two, and learn something new about your traveling companions. Unfortunately, this book can't be all things to all people, but I tried to have something for everyone. There's kid stuff and adult stuff; things for left-brainers, right-brainers, and half-wits; answers you'll know instantly and some that take some mulling.

I've ordered the sections in near-disorganization so nobody gets tired of too much of a good thing. You can go straight through or skip around to the pages that strike your fancy. Be bold. Be brave. Be creative. And, for goodness' sake, make sure somebody keeps an eye on the gas gauge.

SmiLeage

Begin with the End

The first person spells a word. The second person spells a word that begins with the last letter of the previous word. The third person picks up with the last letter of the second person's word and continues on.

Example:
    The first word might be apple, which ends with an "E."
    The second word must begin with an "E," like elephant.
    The third word must begin with a "T."

If you want to be tricky, try to come up with words that end with unusual letters. No word can be used twice in one game.

SMILEAGE

Tell Me a Story

Using these titles to jog your memory, tell a story that really happened. Or put your imagination to work and create an off-the-cuff tall tale.

- ❋ It Happened on a Sled
- ❋ I Thought I Would Die Before We Got to the Bathroom
- ❋ One Bad Vacation
- ❋ I Think I Encountered an Angel
- ❋ It Happened on a Bus
- ❋ In Spite of It All, I Survived!
- ❋ The Worst Food I've Ever Eaten
- ❋ How I Got This Scar
- ❋ My Weirdest Story from a Wedding
- ❋ A Diabolical Practical Joke
- ❋ Porta-Potty!
- ❋ My Strangest Encounter with a Wild Animal
- ❋ My Most Unusual Relative
- ❋ The Worst Job I've Ever Had

Name That Tune

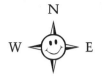

Does the vehicle in which you're traveling have a radio with a "seek" feature? If so, you can play this game easily.

Make sure the volume is loud enough for everyone to hear, and activate the "search." When the radio locks into a station playing music, the first person to name the song being played gets ten points. As soon as someone gives the correct answer, "seek" again. The first person to get one hundred points wins.

N
W E
S

Alphabet Soup

Our world has become an alphabet soup of abbreviations. But there's also plenty of room for confusion. Is a CD a compact disc or certificate of deposit? PMS could be premenstrual syndrome or printer's master scale. PC could be politically correct, personal computer, or public commode.

Come up with real or imaginary possibilities for these letter combinations ASAP.

* OT could mean Overtime or . . .
* DA could mean District Attorney or . . .
* PT could mean Physical Therapy or . . .
* PS could mean Postscript or . . .
* RBI could mean Runs Batted In or . . .
* LD could mean Long Distance or . . .
* JIT could mean Just In Time or . . .
* MS could mean Master of Science or . . .
* RPM could mean Revolutions Per Minute or . . .
* BPS could mean Bytes Per Second or . . .
* VIP could mean Very Important Person or . . .
* ADD could mean Attention Deficit Disorder or . . .

Creative Thinking

- Recast THE WIZARD OF OZ with people you know.
- Make a list of jobs nervous people shouldn't hold.
- If you could have one super power, what would you choose?
- Although you've done nothing wrong, you find that you must hide to avoid being captured by someone who means you harm. Where would you go?
- What five personal items would you put in a time capsule to tell the world something about your life?
- How would your life be affected if the power of magnetism ceased to work?
- You have twenty-four hours to spend one thousand dollars any way you want. What would you do?
- In his book BLUE HIGHWAYS, William Least Heat Moon evaluates the quality of roadside restaurants by the number of calendars on the wall. What criteria would you use to gauge a good diner?
- Come up with a rhyming verse that would precede the line: "My choice, of course, was taxidermy."
- Imagine how your life would have been different yesterday if you were blind.

SMILEAGE

N
W · E
S

Playback

Torturous for those with bad memories, this game operates in a circle. It starts with the first person, continues through to the last, and goes around again. Each person repeats the items all the previous people have said and then adds one with the next letter of the alphabet. When someone fails to recall all the previous items in order, he or she is "out" for that round. The game is played until you complete the category or only one person remains. To make things a little easier, you may want to skip over "Q" and "X." Here is an example using "Professional Athletes":

The first person might say ANDRÉ AGASSI.
The second person might say ANDRÉ AGASSI, LOU BROCK.
The third person might say ANDRÉ AGASSI, LOU BROCK, CHI CHI RODRIGUEZ.

On it goes until you reach "Z."

Here are some categories to get you started:

❋ animals
❋ things you could buy in a mall
❋ colors
❋ birds
❋ famous people
❋ things you would find in a castle
❋ words or phrases you might hear in a hospital
❋ things you would see in an amusement park

N
W E
S

SMILEAGE

Imagination Speculations

Answer each of the following as imaginatively as possible.

Q: How would you know the Pillsbury Doughboy had visited your house?
Example: Someone saw his Rolls in the driveway.

Q: How can you know there's been an elephant in your refrigerator?
Example: Hoofprints in the butter.

Q: Why did the chicken cross the road?
Example: To prove to the armadillo that it could be done.

Q: How many _____ does it take to change a light bulb?
(As in: How many therapists does it take to change a light bulb?)
Example: Only one, but the light bulb really has to want to change.

SMILEAGE

You can also pick on states to express your own prejudices. The 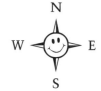 following examples do not necessarily reflect the views of the author:

Q: Why are there no Doberman pinschers in North Dakota?
Example: There's nothing there to guard.

Q: What do they call billboards in Kansas?
Example: Scenery.

Q: What are the two most useless items in Nebraska?
Example: Windows and cameras.

Q: How can you tell they're having a funeral in Alabama?
Example: All the tractors have their lights on.

Cows and Cemeteries

Divide into two teams. The blue team gets the right side of the road; the red team gets the left side of the road. You get one point for every cow on your side of the road. If you pass a cemetery on your side, you drop back to zero and start again. The first team to get to fifty wins. If you're in a cowless area, try the same game with billboards and radio towers or other obvious landmarks.

SMILEAGE

Make Your Own Sequel

When Hollywood finds something that works, it looks for ways to recycle the success by creating series—the STAR WARS trilogy, ROCKY I-VI, FRIDAY THE 13TH, PART 87. Often the sequels aren't as good as the originals. See if you can beat the odds by coming up with strong plots for sequels to these movies:

- E.T.: THE EXTRATERRESTRIAL
- DEAD POETS SOCIETY
- CASABLANCA
- THE COLOR PURPLE
- THE LION KING
- IT'S A WONDERFUL LIFE
- WHEN HARRY MET SALLY . . .
- DANCES WITH WOLVES
- THE SOUND OF MUSIC
- FORREST GUMP
- 101 DALMATIANS

SMILEAGE

Tick, Tick, Tick

You think time passes slowly? Try this: One person watches a clock with a second hand. Each person raises his or her hand to signify when one minute has passed. If you want to keep people from counting one-one-thousand in their heads, make everyone recite the multiplication tables or the Pledge of Allegiance. To really make things slow to a crawl, have everyone hold their breath.

With a Little Help from Their Friends

Working together has been the secret to success for many musical groups. Simon had Garfunkel, Sonny had Cher, and Marky Mark had the Funky Bunch. See if you know who completes this lineup.

- ✸ Tony Orlando and . . .
- ✸ Martha Reeves and . . .
- ✸ Tom Petty and . . .
- ✸ Bill Haley and . . .
- ✸ Gary Puckett and . . .
- ✸ Joan Jett and . . .
- ✸ Tommy James and . . .
- ✸ Kool and . . .

- ✸ Gloria Estefan and . . .
- ✸ The Captain and . . .
- ✸ Sly and . . .
- ✸ Smokey Robinson and . . .
- ✸ Guy Lombardo and . . .
- ✸ Edie Brickell and . . .
- ✸ K. C. and . . .
- ✸ Gladys Knight and . . .

SMILEAGE

Mental Leapfrog

You're probably familiar with association games where one person responds with the first thing that comes to mind when a word is said. This game complicates matters by making a leap across the obvious to the next association.

A person might begin by saying the words BEAN and FORD. The word that went between them was PINTO as in PINTO BEAN and FORD PINTO. Whoever guesses that connection gets to offer the next term.

Example:

The word FORD might be followed by INDIANA JONES. The middle point was HARRISON FORD who played INDIANA JONES.

The next response might be BILLY GRAHAM because both INDIANA JONES and BILLY GRAHAM have CRUSADES in common.

As you can see, any logical connection will do. The fun is in figuring out how someone connected two thoughts. See how far afield you can go before looping back to your original word.

A Little Chat about This and That

- What's been your favorite costume for Halloween or a masquerade party?
- Where's the windiest place you've ever been?
- Who makes the absolute best hamburger?
- Who carries the most keys of anyone you know?
- If you could have a wild animal as a pet, what would you choose?
- Tell a story about a time when a car died.
- What's a package you couldn't wait to receive?
- What TV game show would you be most likely to win?
- If someone gave you two roundtrip airline tickets to fly anywhere in the world, where would you go?
- What's the most amazing magic trick you have ever seen?
- Who has the greatest job of all?
- Where is the quietest place you've ever been?
- If you were offered a makeover with a hairstylist and clothes designer, would you accept it? What do you think these experts would want to change about you?

SMILEAGE

N
W ─●─ E
S

State Nicknames

Every state has a slogan or phrase that uniquely identifies it. Make the people at the Department of Tourism happy by naming the state that goes with each of these:

* Volunteer State
* Garden State
* Green Mountain State
* Cornhusker State
* Show Me State
* Gopher State
* Last Frontier
* Land of Lincoln
* Pelican State
* Bay State
* Evergreen State
* Lone Star State
* Old Dominion
* Silver State

Music to Your Ears

* What are the corniest songs you've ever heard?
* What are the saddest songs of all time?
* What song's lyrics say a lot to you?
* What's the most romantic song you've ever heard?
* If you were going to spend the rest of your life on an island, what ten albums would you take?
* What song is most likely to make you cry?
* What's a great song for driving?
* What song reminds you of last summer?
* What song's lyrics did you totally misunderstand?
* What song would you like to never hear again?
* What song reminds you of someone you have previously dated?
* What is the first song you remember listening to on the radio?
* What are some songs you think are perfect?

Quotable Movies: The Classics

Identify each film by its famous quote.

* "Teacher says, 'Every time a bell rings, an angel gets its wings.'"
* "Listen to the children of the night. What music they make."
* "After all, tomorrow is another day."
* "Don't be so sure I'm as crooked as I'm supposed to be."
* "Play it, Sam. Play 'As Time Goes By.'"
* "Rosebud."
* "My mother thanks you, my father thanks you, my sister thanks you—and I thank you."
* "I coulda had class. I coulda been a contender."
* "I'll be around in the dark. I'll be everywhere—wherever you can look."
* "Miss Jean Louise, stand up. Your father's passin'."
* "I wrestled with reality for forty-five years, doctor, and I'm happy. I finally won over it."
* "Fasten your seat belts, it's going to be a bumpy night."
* "My heart is a bargain today. Will you have me?"

- ❋ "I want to be alone."
- ❋ "No smokey, no talky."
- ❋ "I could dance with you till the cows come home. Better still, I'll dance with the cows and you come home."
- ❋ "The strains of Verdi will come back to you tonight, and Mrs. Claypool's check will come back to you in the morning."
- ❋ "One morning I shot an elephant in my pajamas. How he got into my pajamas I'll never know."
- ❋ "If I ever go looking for my heart's desire again, I won't look any farther than my own backyard."

Who Am I?

See how many of the five clues you need to identify each of these well-known people.

1. I was born in a London slum in 1889.
2. I began my career as a music hall entertainer and eventually became a film actor.
3. By age thirty-three, I had appeared in seventy-one movies.
4. I played the title character in THE GREAT DICTATOR, which was also my first speaking role.
5. Although I eventually started a major motion picture studio, I'm best known as "The Little Tramp."

1. I was born on December 15 or 16, 1770, in Bonn, Germany.
2. By the age of 14, I was working as a court organist.
3. Mozart praised my talents and I studied under Joseph Haydn.
4. When I began to lose my hearing, I removed the legs of my piano so I could feel the vibration through the floor as I composed.
5. Called the Emancipator of Music, I am perhaps best known for my Fifth Symphony.

1. I was born in Atchison, Kansas, in 1897.
2. I studied at Columbia University for a time but dropped out to take flying lessons.
3. I was the first female passenger on a transatlantic flight.
4. I was the first woman to fly across the Atlantic Ocean alone.
5. My plane disappeared over the Pacific Ocean as I attempted to fly around the world.

1. I was born in 1451, the son of a Genoan wool-weaver.
2. Although I had little schooling, I loved to spend time learning about ships at the port.
3. In 1477, I came to Lisbon, Portugal, where my brother ran a shop that sold nautical instruments and maps.
4. I believed that I could find a fast route to the Indies by sailing west.
5. In 1492, I set out for a great adventure with three ships—the Niña, the Pinta, and the Santa Maria.

SMILEAGE

TV Trivia

- Name the eatery where the Fonz and Richie Cunningham hung out.
- What did the Cartwrights call their ranch on Bonanza?
- Name Samantha's sometimes-wicked witch mother on BEWITCHED.
- What show featured the misadventures of Ralph and Alice Kremden?
- Clint Eastwood played Rowdy Yates on what western?
- Name the detective played by Jack Lord on HAWAII FIVE-O.
- What was the actual name of the hospital nicknamed ST. ELSEWHERE?
- What show featured young ultra-conservative Alex P. Keaton?
- Name the car that the Dukes of Hazzard drove.
- Where does Homer Simpson work?
- THE PHIL SILVERS SHOW is also known by two other titles. Name them.
- Name Dr. Frasier Crane's icy ex-wife.
- What did the Clampetts of THE BEVERLY HILLBILLIES call their swimming pool?

* What character did THE FUGITIVE dedicate his life to apprehending?
* THE CAROL BURNETT SHOW frequently featured a soap opera parody. Name it.
* Who hosted PASSWORD for many years?
* What series followed the lives of the Huxtables?
* What duo hosted LAUGH-IN?
* Ed Ames played a Cherokee named Mingo in what frontier series?
* Willie Aames played Dick Van Patten's son on what family-oriented series?
* Name the town where the Ingalls lived on LITTLE HOUSE ON THE PRAIRIE.
* Name Maxwell Smart's female sidekick on GET SMART!
* What newscaster ended his report with the trademark phrase "And that's the way it is . . ."?
* Name the Frankensteinlike butler on THE ADDAMS FAMILY.

N
W E
S

Animal Riddles

* Where does an elephant pack his peanuts?
* Why doesn't the turtle wear a tie?
* What does Mama Bear make her babies for dessert?
* What do you call little dogs when they get cold?
* What else can you call them?
* What do little Australian bears like to drink?
* How do chickens measure how much food they eat?
* Why can't the ducks go to sleep?
* What would you call a person who can rid you of rabbits?
* What would you receive from a polite snake after it bites you?

Stuff to Talk About

* Where're the hottest and coldest places you've ever been?
* Most license plates are a combination of seven letters and numbers. If you were going to order a personalized license plate, what would it say? (e.g., CRE8, QTPIE, 10ISPRO)
* You know you're in a small town when . . .
* The word STRIKE has over two dozen meanings. How many can you come up with?
* What is the greatest invention of all time? Of the twentieth century?
* What crime would you be most likely to mastermind?
* Where did Jason in Friday the 13th get his hockey mask?
* Why do some small towns have traffic lights where the red and yellow lights are on simultaneously?
* One of the most popular first names in recent history is Michael. How many famous Michaels can you name?
* Add to this list of dubious highway promises: "Conveniently located . . . ," "only minutes from . . . ," "the world's largest. . ."
* All the animals at the zoo are running loose. What creature do you least want to encounter?

SMILEAGE

Two Truths, One Lie

All participants come up with two true statements and one fabrication about themselves. Each person has the opportunity to tell his or her two truths and one lie. Then all the listeners voice their opinions on which one is bogus.

Here are three examples I've used:

- ✱ I've written a script in which Roy Rogers makes a guest appearance.
- ✱ I once rode in a van for twenty-eight hours without falling asleep.
- ✱ I sat next to film critic Roger Ebert at a movie screening.

In this case, the third statement is false. I was formerly a staff writer for a cable TV sitcom that featured Roy Rogers in an episode, and I was so excited about snow skiing in Colorado I couldn't relax enough to sleep.

The Big Quiz

N
W E
S

The answer to each of the following clues has the word big in it. Have a large time coming up with the right response.

* nickname of New Orleans
* tall yellow cast member of Sesame Street
* famous sandwich at restaurant founded by Ray Kroc
* nickname for Montana
* creepy all-knowing character in George Orwell's 1984
* TV series starring Barbara Stanwick as Victoria Barkley
* 1971 western starring John Wayne and Richard Boone
* artist who originally recorded "Chantilly Lace"
* postulates that the world was formed as the result of a huge explosion
* nickname for New York City
* synonym for a circus tent
* name of the bell in the clock tower at the House of Parliament
* name of the huge cannon used to shell Paris in 1918
* mythical gorillalike creature also known as Sasquatch

SMILEAGE

Just My Imagination

- How would you have gotten off of Gilligan's Island?
- What would it have been like to be going where you're headed now in a covered wagon or on horseback?
- A genie is about to grant you three wishes. What would they be?
- If you were an animal, what would you be?
- If you had to spend the rest of your life with the characters in a TV show, what program would you choose to be in?
- If you could live in any period of history, what would you choose?
- If the television news show 60 MINUTES calls you, what would you suspect that they'd like to talk to you about?
- What event in your life was so befuddled that it resembled the work of The Three Stooges or Lucy and Ethel?
- What's an unusual food combination you like?
- If you were going to open a retail store, what kind of merchandise would you sell?
- TIME magazine has just named you "Man of the Year" or "Woman of the Year." What would be their reason for bestowing upon you this honor?

Quotable Movies: The '60s

Identify each film by the famous quote.

⊛ "Whistles are for dogs and certainly not for children."
⊛ "I wouldn't hurt a fly."
⊛ "Supercalifragilisticexpialidocious."
⊛ "Well, come see a fat old man sometime."
⊛ "Rumble!"
⊛ "All the facts about you are insults."
⊛ "I just wanna ride my machine without being hassled by the man."
⊛ "I can no longer sit back and allow Communist infiltration, Communist indoctrination, Communist subversion, and the international Communist conspiracy to sap and impurify our precious bodily fluids."
⊛ "I'm sorry, Dave. I'm afraid I can't do that."

N
W   E
S

License Plate Bingo

Each player picks a five-letter word and announces it to his or her opponents. You mark off letters of your word when you find them on license plates. Other opponents can use the same letters— no need to argue over who saw something first.

Example:

If your word was PUTTY, you can mark off one "T" when you see a car with license XTL-835. You're left with "P-U-T-Y." If the next car's plate is CM-8392, you make no progress. If the third car's license reads 932-YMU, you can mark off the "Y" and the "U."

The first person to find all his or her letters wins.

Name Three Famous People

Spelling doesn't count in this little game of association. Come up with names that remind you of the following:

- ❀ birds
  Examples: actor Ethan Hawke, basketball player Larry Bird, actor Gregory Peck
- ❀ fruits and vegetables
  Examples: Harlem Globetrotter Meadowlark Lemon, baseball player Daryl Strawberry, comedian Orson Bean
- ❀ colors
- ❀ animals
- ❀ cities
- ❀ plants and trees
- ❀ fish
- ❀ military
- ❀ professions
- ❀ music
- ❀ boats

N
W — E
S

Think Fast

    In the movie SPEED, a city bus has been wired to explode if it goes below fifty miles per hour. Imagine that you've learned that the vehicle in which you're traveling has been similarly rigged. In order to save your lives, what do you do?

Fun Conversations

⊛ What's the funniest joke you can remember?

⊛ What food do you hate the most?

⊛ Describe the worst arts-and-crafts creation you've ever seen.

⊛ In what Olympic event would you be most likely to compete?

⊛ What are the strangest real names of people you've heard?

⊛ What's the best way to annoy you?

⊛ If you were given a gift certificate for plastic/cosmetic surgery, would you use it? If so, how?

⊛ What's the longest play or musical program you've endured?

⊛ What's the nicest hotel room you've ever stayed in?

⊛ What's a line from a song you find particularly meaningful?

⊛ Who was your favorite teacher?

⊛ What's your most embarrassing moment in life?

⊛ What accomplishment in your life are you most proud of?

⊛ What would you want inscribed on your tombstone?

Points of Interest

From coast to coast, America has points of interest of every size—from the internationally known Grand Canyon right down to the Boll Weevil Monument in Enterprise, Alabama. Here are some unique (though lesser known) actual tourist attractions. Add to this list with your own curious discoveries.

- ✸ World's Largest Ball of Twine—Darwin, Minnesota
  The name sort of says it all, except its ever-growing size—over 21,000 pounds and 12 feet in circumference.
- ✸ Liars' Hall of Fame—Dannebrog, Nebraska
  Tired of stuffy museums? Try this tongue-in-cheek center that promotes America's second most popular indoor sport.
- ✸ Teapot Dome Service Station—near Zillah, Washington
  It's an actual working gas station built to resemble—you guessed it—a teapot as a protest of the 1921 oil scandal that rocked President Warren G. Harding's administration.
- ✸ Checkers Hall of Fame—Petal, Mississippi
  The crowning achievement of Charles C. Walker's devotion to his favorite pastime, you'll find boards of every variety as well as checkered patterns on everything imaginable.

SMILEAGE

- Underwear of the Stars Museum—Houston, Texas
  Tell all your friends you've gazed upon unmentionables formerly worn by Madonna, Muhammad Ali, Sting, and Elvira, among others.
- Wigwam Village—Holbrook, Arizona and Cave City, Kentucky
  Did Native Americans really build teepees of concrete equipped with Magic Fingers vibrating beds the way this historic roadside motel might have you believe?
- South of the Border—Dillon, South Carolina
  A fiesta for the eyes including enormous concrete animals and semi-magnificent Sombrero Tower.
- World's Largest Frying Pan—Rose Hill, North Carolina
  Again, the name seems to tell the whole story.
- Area 51—Roswell, New Mexico
  No one really knows what's there, but if you get in and get back out, please let us in on the secret.

Either/Or Lifestyles

Contemporary culture craves choices, but what do you pick when you only have two options? See what the following choices reveal about your traveling companions.

Would you rather . . .

⊛ live in a Manhattan penthouse or a Montana ranch house?
⊛ drive a taxi or operate a toll booth?
⊛ take a picnic to the park or dine in a fine restaurant?
⊛ live where it's always warm and rainy or cold and dry?
⊛ attend a rodeo or an art exhibition?
⊛ stay at a hotel with a health club or one with 130 cable channels?
⊛ live in a house where you've spotted mice or roaches?
⊛ do telephone sales or work at a used car lot?
⊛ own a home with a state-of-the-art entertainment center or an indoor pool?
⊛ hire a maid or a personal fitness trainer?
⊛ live where it's 78 degrees and sunny year round or experience the changes of four seasons?

SMILEAGE

- drive a convertible or a four-wheel-drive vehicle?
- get by for a week without toothpaste or shampoo?
- receive fifty thousand dollars a year for life or a one-time check for five hundred thousand dollars?
- tour the country in a private bus or a sportscar?
- go without breakfast or lunch?
- own an apartment complex or an office building?
- work in an environment that's noisy or smelly?
- forget to wear a belt or have a noticeable stain on your shirt?

SMILEAGE

Tell Me Another Story

Here is a veritable smorgasbord of titles. Tell a memory or make a story that fits the topic.

- ⊛ Weird Weather
- ⊛ Runaway Car
- ⊛ While Climbing a Tree
- ⊛ Planes, Trains, or Automobiles
- ⊛ . . . And Then I Threw Up
- ⊛ It Happened at the Zoo
- ⊛ The Not-So-Great Outdoors
- ⊛ Learning to Ride a Bike
- ⊛ They Warned Me Not To
- ⊛ The Perils of Skiing
- ⊛ The Worst Bathroom I've Ever Encountered
- ⊛ Some Things Just Don't Want to Be Fixed
- ⊛ It Happened at the Hospital
- ⊛ One Really Wild Roller Coaster
- ⊛ Just About the Worst Night of My Life

Spinoffs

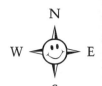

Through the years, successful (and not-so-successful) TV shows have often introduced characters that go on to helm their own series. Can you name the programs that begat these shows?

* RHODA
* LOU GRANT
* PHYLLIS
* FRASIER
* JOANIE LOVES CHACHI
* MORK AND MINDY
* TRAPPER JOHN, M.D.
* THE FACTS OF LIFE

* KNOT'S LANDING
* THE HONEYMOONERS
* GOMER PYLE, USMC
* THE JEFFERSONS
* MAUDE
* GOOD TIMES
* LAVERNE AND SHIRLEY

Playing Favorites

Get into any small group and they're likely to have an activity where they ask your favorite color and your favorite food. There's a whole world that has gone untapped . . . until now.

What's your . . .

* favorite flavor of ice cream?
* favorite Monopoly property and game piece?
* favorite photograph?
* favorite shirt?
* favorite meal?
* favorite activity for a rainy day?
* favorite way to spend Sunday afternoon?
* favorite place to relax?
* favorite color in a sixty-four-box of Crayolas?
* favorite book as a child?
* favorite time of day?
* favorite board game?
* favorite breakfast?

- favorite store?
- favorite place to take a walk?
- favorite sport to play?
- favorite sport to watch on TV?
- favorite cast member from the twenty-five-plus years of SATURDAY NIGHT LIVE?
- favorite Muppet?
- favorite place to watch the sunset?
- favorite sandwich and the instructions to make it perfectly?
- favorite shoes?
- favorite memory from childhood?

Beemer Bummer

If you're in a wealthy area, this game could become frustrating, but try it anyway if you're good at identifying cars. Each person chooses a make of automobile (Nissan, Ford, Chevrolet, etc.) and scores a point for every one he or she spots. If someone spots a BMW (or Beemer), the person announces "Beemer Bummer." Everyone loses his or her points and starts again. Unless you're in a highly trafficked area, the goal is fifty points.

Hail to This Chief Quiz

Name the U.S. President associated with each key phrase.

- The New Deal
- "A kinder, gentler America"
- The Great Depression
- Emancipation Proclamation
- The Square Deal
- New Frontier
- Louisiana Purchase
- "He kept us out of war"
- Voodoo economics
- "Building a bridge to the twenty-first century"
- "Time for a change."
- "Let the people rule."

Discuss and Debate

⊛ Should the toilet paper roll over the top or drop from behind?

⊛ Answer the question posed in the movie STAND BY ME: "Mickey's a mouse, Donald's a duck. What's Goofy?"

⊛ Should Puerto Rico become the fifty-first state of the Union?

⊛ Was the three-point field goal in basketball a good idea?

⊛ Why is there no aspirin in Aspercreme?

⊛ Some have said that the national anthem is too hard to sing. Should "The Star-Spangled Banner" be replaced? If so, is there a song that you would recommend?

⊛ Just how much law enforcement authority do patrol mothers really have?

⊛ If an apple a day keeps the doctor away, what does half an apple do?

⊛ What do you think has been done with the tissue removed from Michael Jackson's nose?

⊛ Has the designated hitter rule improved the game of baseball?

⊛ Which came first: the chicken or the egg?

⊛ Some believe that learning a second language should be a mandatory school requirement. Do you agree?

The Moral of the Story Is . . .

Aesop had his fables. Jesus had his parables. Confucius had his sayings. Solomon had his proverbs. Come up with stories that will end with "It just goes to show that . . ."

* the grass isn't always greener on the other side.
* you should make hay while the sun shines.
* what goes around comes around.
* you can't always get what you want.
* not everything that glitters is gold.
* two heads are better than one.
* you don't know a good thing till it's gone.
* you had better be careful what you wish for.
* you can't please all of the people all of the time.

SMILEAGE

The Game Is A to Z

Try this simple alphabet game that's fun for any age. Someone announces, "The game is A to Z. The category is ____" and fills in the blank.

Example:

If the category is Animals, the answers might be anteater, baboon, cow, and so on through the alphabet.

You may want to jump over the pesky letters of "Q," "X," and "Z" in some categories—but don't give up without trying. Here are some categories to get you started:

- flowers
- trees
- baseball players
- rock groups
- cars
- colors
- people you know

- TV shows
- things you would find at a circus
- diseases
- foods
- restaurants and stores
- characters in literature

The Name of the Game

The keys to a successful game show are unique gimmicks, grand prizes, and a distinctive vocabulary that sets it apart from all the others. If you heard these phrases, identify the show you'd be watching.

* "I'll take Paul Lynde to block."
* "Bachelor Number Two: If you were a fruit, what kind would you be? And why?
* "Number eighteen and number twenty-six—it's a match."
* "I'd like to buy a vowel."
* "Quotable Quotes for one hundred."
* "Where's the most unusual place you and your wife have made whoopie?"
* "Or you can trade for the box that Jay is bringing down the aisle."
* "C'mon down!"
* "Survey says . . ."
* "The category is 'Things You Would Find in a Kitchen.' Ready? Begin."

Sound Connections

Sometimes a sound triggers a memory of a specific time and place. What comes to mind when you think of these?

- jingle bells
- pipe organ
- train whistle
- water lapping against a boat or dock
- marching band
- cannon blast
- firecrackers
- crackling fire
- crashing waves
- screen door slamming
- streetcar
- jackhammer
- whistling winds
- calliope

Two-Door, Four-Door

Each person picks a vehicle color that he or she will be looking for—blue, white, red, etc. To keep things even, combine black with gray, beige and tan with brown, teal with green. You get twenty points for each two-door car or truck and forty points for each four-door. Hatchbacks don't earn you extra points. The first person to reach five hundred points wins.

N

W ⊕ E

S

Riddle Crossings

- ⊛ What do you get when you cross a sheep and a ten-speed?
- ⊛ What do you get when you cross a dime with three nickels?
- ⊛ What do you get when you cross a cow and a germ?
- ⊛ What do you get if you cross a witch and a waiter?
- ⊛ What do you get when you cross a balloon and a porcupine?
- ⊛ What do you get when you cross a rooster and a pack of gum?
- ⊛ What do you get when you cross a rooster and a cow?
- ⊛ What do you get if you cross a worm and a hook?
- ⊛ What do you get if you cross a chicken and a shrub?
- ⊛ What do you get if you cross a parrot and a mime?
- ⊛ What do you get if you cross a baseball bat and a soft drink?
- ⊛ What do you get if you cross a clown and a mathematician?

Tap

Maybe sometime you've hummed songs for people to "name that tune." If you're tone-deaf and otherwise musically challenged, here's a less stressful alternative. Tap out the beats on your leg or the seat loud enough for everyone to hear and see who will be the first to identify the song. Whoever guesses correctly is the next tapper. If it is too difficult for your crew, confine your songs to one category such as patriotic songs, Christmas carols, hymns, show-tunes, or Randy Travis hits.

Make a List—The Sequel

Much more fun than grocery lists but maybe not as clever as David Letterman's Top Ten. Here's a chance to get in on the act by making your own lists.

- strangest bumper stickers you've seen
- sounds you find irritating
- signs of cheap hotels
- favorite books
- worst jobs imaginable
- greatest cars of all time
- terrible names for sports teams
- greatest homes you've ever seen
- annoying behaviors of other drivers
- ugliest clothes you've owned
- funniest people (friends or celebrities)
- smartest pets
- biggest rip-offs

Quotable Movies: The '70s

Identify each film by the famous quote.

* "Bring me a shrubbery."
* "Trust the force, Luke."
* "What in the wide, wide world of sports is going on here?"
* "Frau Bluecher!"
* "You've got to ask yourself one question: Do I feel lucky?"
* "I lost my ID in a flood and I was wondering, would you pick me up some Old Harper's hard stuff?"
* "Who are those guys?"
* "I'm gonna make him an offer he can't refuse."
* "Love means never having to say you're sorry."
* "Make my day."
* "You talkin' to me? You talkin' to me?"
* "La-di-da. La-di-da."
* "Adrian! A-dri-an!"

SMILEAGE

Geography Quiz

- Which four U.S. states border Mexico?
- Eight states begin with the letter "M." Name them.
- Name the five states that have a Pacific coastline.
- Five states have a coastline on the Gulf of Mexico. Name them.
- Which state claims to be the Mother of Presidents because eight U.S. presidents were born there?
- Five state capitals begin with the letter "A." How many can you name?
- Which of the forty-eight continental states has the northernmost point?
- The Mississippi River provides a state line for which ten states?
- Alaska and Texas are the two largest states in the union. What's number 3?
- Alaska and Hawaii were the last two states to be added to the union. What was number 48?
- Eight state capitals are two-word names. How many can you recall?
- Tennessee is bordered by eight states. Name them.
- Which state has the highest ratio of airplanes to people?

Talking Topics

* What's the longest you've gone without a bath?
* What's the wildest roller coaster you've ever ridden?
* What cartoon character are you most like?
* What would make a good name for a band?
* Who should be in prison but isn't?
* What is your all-time favorite birthday present?
* If you wrote a book, what would it be about?
* What would you have named yourself?
* What accomplishment in your life are you most proud of?
* If you were going to participate in a protest or picket line, what cause would you be supporting or opposing?
* If you could have dinner with any three people who've ever lived, who would you choose?
* Who do you know who consistently practices the Golden Rule of doing unto others as you would have them do unto you?
* Describe your life in ten years.
* What's something that people rarely ask you about that you'd like to talk about more?

SMILEAGE

Cinematic Common Threads

When you think of the Empire State Building, what movie comes to mind? KING KONG? AN AFFAIR TO REMEMBER? SLEEPLESS IN SEATTLE? Let me provide you with some standard settings, characters, or scenes—you come up with a movie that fits the bill.

- ⊛ locker room pep talk
- ⊛ delivery room of a hospital
- ⊛ blowing out the candles on a birthday cake
- ⊛ tracing a phone call
- ⊛ crawling through a duct
- ⊛ playing a jukebox
- ⊛ a person with amnesia
- ⊛ takes place during a single day
- ⊛ a southern sheriff
- ⊛ climactic courtroom scene
- ⊛ tearful farewell
- ⊛ characters running through fire
- ⊛ a hero trying to diffuse a bomb ticking down to zero
- ⊛ fireworks display

- high school gymnasium
- an actor playing multiple characters
- characters with funny accents or speech patterns
- elevator
- a zoo
- computer expert trying to break a code
- an autopsy being performed
- a swimming pool
- a subway station
- a drawbridge raising
- shooting a lock with a pistol
- walking on a beach
- dramatic speech before dying

N
W ☺ E
S

Initial Responses

All of the following literary works were written by authors who are known by their initials instead of their given names. Can you identify them by their most notable works?

* WAR OF THE WORLDS
* THE LORD OF THE RINGS
* CHARLOTTE'S WEB
* THE CATCHER IN THE RYE
* GOOSEBUMPS
* THE OUTSIDERS
* OLD POSSUM'S BOOK OF PRACTICAL CATS
* THE LION, THE WITCH, AND THE WARDROBE
* WINNIE THE POOH

The Stooge Way

N

W E

S

If you're The Three Stooges, you don't need fancy dental devices to pull a tooth—just a hammer, a pair of pliers, and maybe a string tied to a doorknob. Imagine how Larry, Curly, and Moe would do the following:

- ✸ remove contact lenses
- ✸ disarm a nuclear weapon
- ✸ install computer software
- ✸ prepare for a tornado to touch down
- ✸ perform microsurgery
- ✸ dislodge Santa Claus from a chimney
- ✸ operate an air traffic control center
- ✸ capture a bull in a china shop

Please . . . Just One More Story

Take the title and supply the content. If you're stumped with fact, go with fiction.

- ⊛ Fun with Electricity
- ⊛ The Best Letter I've Ever Received
- ⊛ One Awkward Situation
- ⊛ It Happened in a Restaurant
- ⊛ A Sick Experience with a Doctor
- ⊛ Falling Down and Going Boom
- ⊛ The Photograph I'd Like to Burn
- ⊛ A Big Thought from a Little Kid
- ⊛ Love Story
- ⊛ It Was Like Something Out of a Movie
- ⊛ I Thought I Knew What I Was Doing
- ⊛ Major Rip-Off
- ⊛ A Lesson in Being Grateful
- ⊛ It Was a Miracle

Where Were You When . . . ?

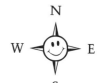

If you're forty, you probably don't remember much about the Great Depression (unless that's what you call the period after the breakup with your high school sweetheart). The following are notable events of the past fifty years. If you were around, describe where you were and what you remember about these fateful days.

* the assassination of President Kennedy
* the astronauts' walk on the moon
* the L.A. riots following the Rodney King trial
* Elvis's death (if, in fact, he has departed)
* TV reports of the bombing of Baghdad
* live coverage of O. J. Simpson riding in the white Bronco
* the Beatles's appearance on THE ED SULLIVAN SHOW
* the assassination attempt on President Reagan
* John Lennon's death
* Tiny Tim and Miss Vicki's wedding on THE TONIGHT SHOW

SMILEAGE

Just Duet

Can you identify the artists who performed these duets?

- ❋ "Foggy Mountain Breakdown" (1968)
- ❋ "Don't Go Breaking My Heart" (1976)
- ❋ "The Sounds of Silence" (1966)
- ❋ "Beauty and the Beast" (1992)
- ❋ "(I've Had) the Time of My Life" (1987)
- ❋ "Then Came You" (1974)
- ❋ "Walk This Way" (1986)
- ❋ "You Don't Have to Be a Star (To Be in My Show)" (1977)
- ❋ "On My Own" (1986)
- ❋ "Ebony and Ivory" (1982)
- ❋ "Say, Say, Say" (1983)
- ❋ "Unforgettable" (1991)
- ❋ "I Got You Babe" (1965)
- ❋ "Islands in the Stream" (1983)
- ❋ "Next Time I Fall" (1986)
- ❋ "You Don't Bring Me Flowers" (1978)
- ❋ "Up Where We Belong" (1982)

- "Endless Love" (1981)
- "You're the One That I Want" (1978)
- "Ya Mo B There" (1984)
- "Somethin' Stupid" (1967)
- "You're All I Need To Get By" (1968)
- "Don't Fall in Love with a Dreamer" (1980)
- "Louisiana Woman, Mississippi Man" (1973)
- "Too Much, Too Little, Too Late" (1978)
- "Somewhere Out There" (1987)
- "Cryin' (Crying)" (1987)
- "We're Gonna Hold On" (1973)
- "I'm Gonna Make You Love Me" (1968)

The Little Quiz

No, it's not much shorter than any of the other brain-ticklers in this book but all the answers have to have the word little in them. Small wonder, huh?

- ❋ book by Laura Ingalls Wilder and the series from Michael Landon
- ❋ site of General George Armstrong Custer's last stand
- ❋ most famous novel by Louisa May Alcott
- ❋ capital of Arkansas
- ❋ children's book written by Frances Hodgson Burnett about a young girl
- ❋ children's book written by Frances Hodgson Burnett about a young boy
- ❋ 1963 car song by the Beach Boys
- ❋ play and movie that tell the story of a talking, singing, man-eating plant
- ❋ cartoon strip set in Dogpatch, U.S.A.
- ❋ one of Robin Hood's Merry Men
- ❋ very "clean" song recorded by the Jarmels in 1961

SMILEAGE

- constellation at the end of which is the North Star
- baseball organization for minors
- outlandish singer known for hits including "Tutti Fruitti" and "Good Golly Miss Molly"
- name for the mischievous kids of the OUR GANG comedies
- curly-haired comic strip character with a dog named Sandy
- Shirley Temple movie in which she is left as collateral on a gambling debt
- animated Disney movie that takes place under the sea
- fairy tale about a resourceful little girl who takes a basket of goodies to her grandmother's house

N
W E
S

SMILEAGE

N
W   E
S

Oxygen

A breathtaking twist on find-the-letter games, Oxygen can be played in two forms using the same basic rules. The objective is to find the letters in the word oxygen on billboards, license plates, street signs—wherever you look. The trick is that all players must hold their breath at the same time and point to the letters in order.

Someone says "on your mark, get set," and then everyone takes a breath. Each person searches without breathing until someone says "Got it!" To win, the person must tell the other players where he or she found each letter: "The 'O' was in the license plate of the blue car that just passed us, the 'X' was on the exit sign. . . ."

A noisier variation can be played by dividing the group into teams of two. One person is the looker; the other is the teller. The looker holds his or her breath and points until the teller is able to say where the looker has found the next letter: "You see 'O' in 'Holiday' on the Holiday Inn billboard." The looker nods if that is correct and moves to the next letter. To keep things fair, you may need to appoint one person to serve as referee.

Don't play this game where there is limited signage or little traffic—somebody could pass out.

Make a List—Hollywood Style

"A critic," wrote Kenneth Tynan in THE NEW YORK TIMES MAGAZINE, "is a man who knows the way but can't drive the car." As you're traveling along, here's your chance to play Siskel or Ebert.

- List your top ten all-time favorite movies.
- What are the three worst movies you've ever seen?
- What's the biggest tearjerker you've ever sobbed through?
- What single scene in a movie made you cry?
- What's the greatest adventure movie of all time?
- What's the smartest movie you've seen?
- Who are the five movie villains you most love to hate?
- What are your favorite Disney movies?
- What do you consider the funniest movie scenes of all time?

Did You See the One . . . ?

Take this opportunity to talk about your favorite episodes of these popular TV shows:

* THE ANDY GRIFFITH SHOW
* M*A*S*H*
* NIGHT GALLERY/TWILIGHT ZONE
* STAR TREK (the original or any of its successors)
* SEINFELD
* THE MARY TYLER MOORE SHOW
* CHEERS
* THE X-FILES
* WILD, WILD WEST
* NORTHERN EXPOSURE
* MISSION:IMPOSSIBLE
* HILL STREET BLUES
* ALFRED HITCHCOCK PRESENTS
* ALL IN THE FAMILY
* MORK AND MINDY

Where in the World Would You Be . . . ?

Using these clues, identify the country you would be visiting if you were . . .

- ✹ having lunch in Beijing
- ✹ visiting the Great Pyramids
- ✹ climbing Mount Everest
- ✹ sailing from the Rock of Gibraltar
- ✹ in a land where kiwis abound but no snakes
- ✹ ordering a vegamite sandwich
- ✹ entering a country formerly known as Rhodesia
- ✹ touring the plant where the Porsche was originally manufactured
- ✹ speeding down the Autobahn
- ✹ gazing up from the base of Mount Fuji
- ✹ standing atop a fjord
- ✹ admiring the Taj Mahal
- ✹ hiking up Mount Kilimanjaro

N
W   E
S

Breaking Out in Song

Sing every song you can recall that has the following words:

- ❀ bus
- ❀ train
- ❀ plane or airplane
- ❀ suitcase
- ❀ driving
- ❀ travel
- ❀ highway
- ❀ interstate
- ❀ road

For an added challenge, see how many songs you can come up with that mention specific makes or models of cars.

Examples:
"In My Merry Oldsmobile"
"GTO"
"Little Red Corvette"

It's a Tree but Not a Bush

Once it took the entire drive from Little Rock to Dallas before everyone in the van figured out this little brainteaser. The task is to demonstrate that you know the secret by providing three pairs of correct answers.

Here are three examples:
> It's a tree but not a bush.
> It's Mello Yello but not Mountain Dew.
> It's Nissan but not Ford.

If you think you know the relationship between these sets, turn to the answers in the back of the book. The first person to look becomes the judge for everyone else.

Renaming the Classics

Pretend that the original titles of these movies and TV shows have already been taken. It's your job to rename them.

Example:
I once played this game with a teenager who was told that THE WIZARD OF OZ was already taken. His fast response: "I'd call it GONE WITH THE WIND."

⊛ E.T.: THE EXTRATERRESTRIAL
⊛ TOY STORY
⊛ HOME ALONE
⊛ IT'S A WONDERFUL LIFE
⊛ BATMAN
⊛ JURASSIC PARK
⊛ MIRACLE ON 34TH STREET

⊛ TOP GUN
⊛ JAWS
⊛ FORREST GUMP
⊛ DANCES WITH WOLVES
⊛ BEAUTY AND THE BEAST
⊛ SISTER ACT
⊛ THE WIZARD OF OZ
⊛ GONE WITH THE WIND

Sports Alias

Many high-profile athletes have earned nicknames in their careers. Here are what their fans called them; come up with the names their mamas know them as.

- ⊛ Wilt the Stilt
- ⊛ Refrigerator
- ⊛ Too Tall
- ⊛ Pistol Pete
- ⊛ The Golden Bear
- ⊛ The Iron Horse
- ⊛ Mean Joe
- ⊛ Joltin' Joe
- ⊛ Smokin' Joe
- ⊛ Shoeless Joe
- ⊛ Broadway Joe
- ⊛ FloJo
- ⊛ Stan the Man
- ⊛ Minister of Defense
- ⊛ Dandy Don
- ⊛ The Fearsome Foursome

SMILEAGE

N
W · E
S

Absurd Ponderings

If you're getting a little punchy from too many hours on the road, these suggestions may be just what you need.

* Come up with interesting ways to divide the world into two neat categories. Examples: men/women, right-handed people/lefties, bellybutton innies/outies
* Inexplicably, the number "5" no longer works on any telephones, computers, automatic teller machines, or other devices. How does that change the world?
* Attila the Hun has discovered the ability to travel through time. What is the most absurd situation in which you can imagine him?
* How would your life and the world in general be different if no one ever needed to sleep?
* If the Confederate States decided to once again secede from the United States, what ramifications would there be?
* Imagine that the next town you drive through has a three-story building with no windows and one door on the third floor

with no staircase leading to it. Explain why such an odd structure exists.

⊛ Imagine James Bond in Small Claims Court.

⊛ If suddenly no one in the world could use their thumbs, how would it affect life as we know it?

⊛ A tribe of people who speak an unknown language is discovered in a remote area that will be ravaged by a quick-spreading and deadly airborne virus. What are the first words you want to use to communicate with them?

⊛ It is discovered that aliens captured an adult male from the United States and created one thousand clones who are now dispersed across North America. It is your job to round up these alien creations. You have in your possession a photograph of the human who was abducted. How do you thwart the aliens' plans?

N
W · E
S

Stranded

Your car runs out of gas on an isolated desert road fifty miles from the nearest town at noon. It is unlikely that another car will pass your way for the next twenty-four hours. You have no food or water with you. The temperature is nearing 110 degrees. How do you cope with the situation?

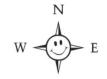

I See Two. Now Do You?

One person chooses two items that start with the same letter then announces, "I see two. Now do you? They both start with the letter __." The objective, of course, is to identify both. They can be anywhere in view. For example, you might use SPEEDOMETER and SHOE or MIRROR and MUFFLER or NOSE and NOTEBOOK.

You can also play the game with colors, but it'll work better if you narrow things down by being specific with terms like light blue, burgundy, or lime green.

Great Beginnings in Literature

Can you identify these literary classics by only the first sentence?

* "It was the best of times, it was the worst of times. . . ."
* "Call me Ishmael."
* "On January 6, 1843, the people of Paris were awakened by the tumultuous clanging of all the bells of the city."
* "Whether I shall turn out to be the hero of my own life, or whether that station will be held by anyone else, these pages must show."
* "'Tom!' No answer. 'Tom!' No answer. 'What's gone with that boy, I wonder? You, Tom!'"
* "It was a bright cold day in April and the clocks were striking thirteen."
* "You will rejoice to hear that no disaster has accompanied the commencement of an enterprise which you have regarded with such evil forebodings."
* "Squire Trelawney, Dr. Livesey, and the rest of these gentlemen have asked me to write down the whole particulars about . . ."

* "Two households, both alike in dignity, in fair Verona."
* "An hour before sunset, on the evening of a day in the beginning of October, 1815, a man travelling afoot entered the little town of D_____."
* "A few miles south of Soledad, the Salinas River drops in close to the hillside bank and runs deep and green."
* "Sunday, 14 June, 1942. On Friday, June 12 I woke up at six o'clock and no wonder; it was my birthday."
* "If you really want to hear about it, the first thing you'll probably want to know is where I was born, and what my lousy childhood was like, and how my parents were occupied and all before they had me, and all that David Copperfield kind of crap, but I don't feel like going into it, if you want to know the truth."

SMILEAGE

N
W • E
S

Quotable Movies: The '80s

Identify each film by its famous quote.

- ❋ "I'll be back."
- ❋ "I have a need for speed."
- ❋ "Demented and sad but social."
- ❋ "You go right back up there and get me a toddler. I need a baby, Hi."
- ❋ "My name is Inego Montoya. You killed my father. Prepare to die."
- ❋ "We're on a mission from God."
- ❋ "You guys are guests in my corn."
- ❋ "I am serious. And don't call me Shirley."
- ❋ "That's not a knife. Now this, this is a knife."
- ❋ "I'm not bad. I'm just drawn that way."
- ❋ "I'm an excellent driver."
- ❋ "There are two kinds of women—high maintenance and low maintenance."
- ❋ "The numbers all go to eleven. Look, right across the board—eleven, eleven, eleven."

- ✸ "I'm not crazy, M'lynn. I've just been in a very bad mood for forty years."
- ✸ "He slimed me."
- ✸ "Norman! The loons! They've come 'round to say good-bye."
- ✸ "Those aren't pillows!"
- ✸ "I want to party with you, cowboy."
- ✸ "Serpentine!"
- ✸ "I am your density."

N
W ⊕ E
S

Horsing Around

Back in the days when Hollywood westerns sat high in the saddle, cowboy actors were well-known for the horses they rode. Can you brand these horses with their owners?

- ❋ Silver
- ❋ Trigger
- ❋ Tony
- ❋ Champion
- ❋ Buttermilk
- ❋ Topper
- ❋ Partner
- ❋ Scout
- ❋ Thunder
- ❋ Diablo
- ❋ Koko

SMILEAGE

84

Here. I'll Give You a Topic. Discuss.

* Where's the most desolate place you've ever been?
* What's the strangest topic you've seen on a TV talk show?
* Where have you seen the most stars?
* Do cellular phones pose a threat to driving safety?
* What's the strangest food you've ever eaten?
* What's the worst junk mail you've received?
* If you were Wile E. Coyote, how would you catch the Roadrunner?
* Where is the most wonderful place you've ever been?
* If you were going to create the perfect breakfast cereal, what would the ingredients be?
* What would you do if you won a million dollars?
* What are your all-time favorite shoes? Why?
* If you were going to be a teacher, what level and subject would you choose?
* What was your favorite toy as a child?
* Should people over age seventy be retested to check their driving skills?
* You have the ability to go back in time and change one event in history. What will you do?

SMILEAGE

N
W E
S

A Collection of Collectors

Sure, you can visit the Smithsonian in Washington, D.C., and all your friends will be impressed. If, however, you want to really get a conversation going, try visiting these learning centers.

* Frog Fantasies Museum—Eureka Springs, Arkansas
  Curators croak about the 5,000+ statues, figurines, sculptures, and ornaments shaped like froggies.
* Carbo's Police Museum—Pigeon Forge, Tennessee
  All sorts of curiosities including Sheriff Buford "Walking Tall" Pusser's "death car."
* Shoe Museum—Philadelphia, Pennsylvania
  A fitting display of footwear from well-heeled celebrities, as well as examples worn by common folk, appropriately displayed by the Pennsylvania College of Podiatric Medicine.
* Liberace Museum—Las Vegas, Nevada
  For those who think too much is never enough, see some of the most outlandish belongings from one of America's flashiest showmen.

- Museum of Beverage Containers—Goodlettsville, Tennessee
  No dorm room has ever amassed a collection that rivals this
  one in my hometown.
- Museum of Questionable Medical Devices—Minneapolis,
  Minnesota
  From equipment that evaluates bumps on your head to electri-
  cal probes purported to stimulate virility, you won't find more
  quackery anywhere.
- Paradise Garden—Summerville, Georgia
  Internationally known folk artist Howard Finister wants to
  have at least one example of every manmade creation at his
  avant-garde park/gallery/museum/junkyard. He hasn't reached
  his goal, but his progress to date is unforgettable.

N
W — E
S

SMILEAGE

You Bet Your Bumper

This won't work if you're driving faster than every other vehicle, so tell the driver to slow down and let other cars pass you. All the players look at the car or truck coming up from behind and bet how many individual bumper stickers, parking decals, and other assorted stick-on materials are on the back of that car.

If you guess correctly, you multiply that score by ten. If you correctly guess zero and there are none, you get ten points. You get no points for overguessing. If you underguessed, you multiply the number you guessed correctly plus individual points for the additonal stickers. Here are some examples to make it easy to follow:

You guessed	There were	Your score
1	0	0
0	0	10
1	2	11 (10 + 1)
1	3	12 (1 x 10 + 2)
3	4	31 (3 x 10 + 1)

The first person to reach two hundred points wins.

Almost Never-Ending Story

Each person has the opportunity to add a new section to a story. The fun is in ending your part so that it taxes the imagination of the person who follows you. Here's just one example:

First person: Once upon a time there was a very brave goatherder who lived in . . .

Second person: . . . Manhattan, which was really an unusual place to herd goats, except that these goats were specially trained to . . .

Third person: . . . sing and dance. They were actually the understudies for roles in the Broadway musical Cats. The reason for their amazing talents was that they were actually . . .

Fourth person: . . . aliens sent here from the planet Goatherdia which is also know for its . . .

You get the idea. Make it simple and straightforward or as absurd as you can get.

SMILEAGE

TV Trivia Too

- What is Hawkeye Pierce's given name?
- Who provided the voice of Charlie for Charlie's Angels?
- Name the carpenter "brothers" from GREEN ACRES.
- What phrase was used on the first few seasons of HILL STREET BLUES to close roll call?
- What ingenious way did the writers bring the show NEWHART to a close?
- What was the Munsters's street address?
- On THE DICK VAN DYKE SHOW, what was the name of Buddy Sorrell's wife?
- Name the rock-throwing hillbilly who made multiple appearances on THE ANDY GRIFFITH SHOW.
- Who shot J. R. on DALLAS?
- Who was the special guest that showed up at Mary Tyler Moore's apartment during a blackout?
- Which child on THE PARTRIDGE FAMILY was played by two different actors?
- Name Carla's ex-husband on CHEERS.
- There were over thirty guest villains on BATMAN. How many can you remember?

SMILEAGE

Something's in the Air

Researchers tell us that the sense of smell can be a powerful trigger for stirring memories. What comes to mind when you get a whiff of these smells?

- cinnamon
- old books
- peppermint
- honeysuckle
- gun powder
- evergreen trees
- fresh mulch
- rubbing alcohol
- rain

- bleach
- strong coffee
- cocoa
- burned toast
- cedar
- musty room
- new carpeting
- scented candles

Two Clues, One Answer

Each of the following pairs has one answer in common. If you
don't guess the answer with the first one, maybe the second one
will help.

- ✸ the ninth planet in the solar system and a Disney dog
- ✸ November's birthstone and an Alfred Hitchcock movie
- ✸ port city in Morocco and a Humphrey Bogart movie
- ✸ unit comprised of two or more military squads and an Oliver
  Stone movie
- ✸ Greek god and the NASA lunar missions
- ✸ July holiday and blockbuster space-invaders movie
- ✸ poker game and a billy club

Now that you've got the idea, add your own twosomes.

C'mon Please . . . One Final, Last Story

If you've read straight through this book, you know what to do. Here are the titles; you supply the story.

* It Happened in a Movie Theater
* One Wacky Neighbor
* Lost!
* Only in My Family
* But What He/She Didn't Know Was . . .
* The Surprise Birthday Party
* I/We Had to Think Quickly
* It Happened in the Woods
* I Thought We'd Never Get Home
* My Most Embarrassing Moment
* I Was So Exhausted
* A Story about a Clown
* The Kindness of Strangers
* It Happened in the Park
* What I Remember from First Grade

SMILEAGE

Deeper Thoughts

- ❋ If you were in the place you feel most relaxed, where would you be?
- ❋ What is one of the most thoughtful acts of kindness done on your behalf?
- ❋ What is the kindest gesture you remember initiating for someone else?
- ❋ Who should we talk to to find out about your best qualities?
- ❋ Who is one of your heroes and why?
- ❋ What attitude in our society bothers you the most?
- ❋ Which of the five senses do you value the most?
- ❋ If someone asked you to name something that has been hard to face, what would you say?
- ❋ What are the telltale signs that you're having a bad day?
- ❋ Who do you wish you were more like?
- ❋ If you could relive any one day of the past year, which would you choose? Why?
- ❋ What would you say has been the best day of your life?
- ❋ What has been the worst day of your life?
- ❋ If you could sum up your philosophy of life in a single sentence, what would it be?

SMILEAGE

Science Test

Experiment with these questions designed to check your scientific knowledge.

⊛ Name the nine planets of our solar system.
⊛ Two-word term that describes the tendency for an object to move outward from the center of a rotating object.
⊛ Thiry-two degrees Fahrenheit is equal to how many degrees Celsius?
⊛ What is the name for the circular glass container in which cultures are grown?
⊛ Animals that are classified as meateaters are given what name?
⊛ What is the layer of atmosphere approximately seven to ten miles above the earth's surface?
⊛ What is the name for the negatively charged part of an atom?
⊛ What element on the periodic table is represented by the symbol "S"?
⊛ In genetics, what word communicates a trait that is the opposite of dominant?
⊛ Name the process by which plants feed by absorbing sunlight.

SMILEAGE

Either/Or Adventures

Given these limited options, which expeditions and pastimes would you choose?

Would you rather . . .

- hike the full length of the Appalachian Trail or sail around the world?
- walk on the moon or deep-sea dive to the Titantic?
- live in medieval England or pioneer-era America?
- ride a burro to the bottom of the Grand Canyon or drive a race car in the Indianapolis 500?
- swim with dolphins or go on a big-game hunt in Africa?
- escape from a prison or weather a hurricane in a small boat?
- visit the Berlin Wall or the Great Wall of China?
- raft down the Snake River or canoe up the Amazon?
- visit the North Pole or an island in the South Seas?
- spend the night alone on a mountaintop or in a cave?
- play in a super-successful band or be moderately successful as a solo artist?

- ski down a glacier or sunbathe in the Caribbean?
- negotiate a peace treaty or lead a revolt against an evil empire?
- be trapped in an elevator for three hours with Regis or Kathie Lee?
- photograph internationally famous models in a studio or natural objects in exotic locations?
- go on an archaeological dig in Israel or explore the surface of Mars in a spacecraft?
- work as a fireman or police officer?
- take lessons in karate or ballroom dancing?

By Any Other Name

Below are the real names of actual and fictional famous people. Do you know the moniker by which we know them best?

* Samuel L. Clemens
* Clark Kent
* Norma Jean Baker
* Theodor Geisel
* Robert Van Winkle
* Lamont Cranston
* Nicholas Coppola
* Frances Gumm
* Roy Scherer
* Gordon Summers
* Caryn Johnson
* Bruce Wayne
* Marion Michael Morrison
* Cherilyn Sarkisian

SMILEAGE

98

In Your Dreams

* What is the strangest dream you've ever had?
* What is the funniest dream you've laughed about?
* What have been your worst nightmares?
* What are your recurring dreams?
* Have your dreams ever come true?
* Do you believe that all dreams have some meaning?
* What's your best story on someone who sleepwalks or talks in his or her sleep?
* Have you had any of these common dreams:
  * being in your underwear or naked in a public place
  * missing a test or important appointment
  * flying without the aid of an airplane or hang glider
  * being paralyzed when you need to move
  * falling a great distance
  * being chased for an unspecified reason
  * being in the company of famous people

SMILEAGE

Quotable Movies: The '90s

Identify each film by its famous quote.

- ⊛ "You can't handle the truth!"
- ⊛ "Did you ever find Bugs Bunny attractive when he put on a dress and played a girl bunny?"
- ⊛ "I'm your number 1 fan."
- ⊛ "Carpe diem. . . . Seize the day. . . . Make your lives extraordinary."
- ⊛ "Come closer, Clarice."
- ⊛ "Tatunka!"
- ⊛ "Houston, we have a problem."
- ⊛ "What I want out of each and every one of you is a hard target search of every gas station, residence, warehouse, farmhouse, henhouse, outhouse, and doghouse in that area."
- ⊛ "Hakuna matada."
- ⊛ "Why, Peter, you've become a pirate."
- ⊛ "The greatest trick the devil ever played was convincing the world that he didn't exist."
- ⊛ "I could've done more."
- ⊛ "Hey, Curly. . . . Kill anyone today?"

Literal Translations

Here are foreign phrases that have made their way into the English language. Can you give the literal interpretation?

* habeas corpus
* a la carte
* e pluribus unum
* au jus
* a la mode
* semper fidelis
* joie de vivre
* c'est la vie
* persona non gratas
* que sera sera
* film noir
* hors d'oeuvre
* hasta la vista
* pro bono
* veni, vidi, vici

Pumpernickel

Great fun for those who like puns and other forms of wordplay. Someone calls out a word, and everyone tries to think of a song lyric that sounds like that word. Some may prove impossible, but don't give up too quickly. Sometimes the hardest ones provide the most creative answers.

A few examples:
* pumpernickel—"PUMPERNICKEL in, in that nickelodeon, all I want is loving you and music, music, music."
  ("Music, Music, Music")
* éclair—"and the rockets ÉCLAIR, the bombs bursting in air"
  ("The Star-Spangled Banner")
* toupee—"he stopped loving her TOUPEE"
  (George Jones's hit "He Stopped Loving Her Today")

Sing the Theme

Very few TV shows have theme songs these days but, through the years, there have been some dandies. See how many are etched in your brain.

- ✴ THE PARTRIDGE FAMILY
- ✴ THE ADDAMS FAMILY
- ✴ FRIENDS
- ✴ THE FLINTSTONES
- ✴ THE JETSONS
- ✴ THE BRADY BUNCH
- ✴ MISTER ROGERS'S NEIGHBORHOOD
- ✴ THE BEVERLY HILLBILLIES
- ✴ CHEERS
- ✴ WELCOME BACK, KOTTER
- ✴ THE MONKEES
- ✴ GREEN ACRES
- ✴ SESAME STREET
- ✴ GILLIGAN'S ISLAND (You knew it had to show up in this book somewhere, didn't you?)

SMILEAGE

Random Topics for Conversation

- What are the worst names you can imagine for a dog or cat?
- If you could spend a day with anyone whose first name is Ed, who would you choose?
- What is the most amazing attraction at an amusement park you've ever experienced?
- In the movie of your life, who should play you?
- Who speaks with the most unusual accent you've heard? Provide an impression of what that person sounds like.
- You know you're sleepy when . . .
- A fight breaks out among all comic book superheroes. It's every man, woman, and creature for himself/herself/itself. Who has the best chance of emerging victorious? Why?
- What are your pet peeves?
- What book should be required reading for everyone in Western civilization?
- What's the tallest building you've ever been in?
- If the place where you live was on fire, what three items would you want to grab on your way out?

- What kind of restaurant would you open?
- What is the single most important item to pack when you're traveling?
- Name the person you believe has the greatest eyes.
- What fad or trend do you consider most foolish?
- What hint would you offer Heloise, the columnist with tips on how to make tasks easier?
- What should be done to keep postal workers from becoming disgruntled and violent?
- What would you consider the brightest idea of your life?
- What's the kindest comment you've heard at a memorial service?

Role Reversals

Actors like to show their range by appearing in movies that are radically different. Here are pairs of movies that have an actor or actress in common. Can you identify the thespian in question?

* RAIDERS OF THE LOST ARK/AMERICAN GRAFFITI
* TO KILL A MOCKINGBIRD/APOCALYPSE NOW
* MIDNIGHT COWBOY/HOOK
* STAND BY ME/JAWS
* THELMA AND LOUISE/DEAD MAN WALKING
* THE TOWERING INFERNO/NAKED GUN
* DRIVING MISS DAISY/THE BLUES BROTHERS
* THE WAY WE WERE/BUTCH CASSIDY AND THE SUNDANCE KID
* IT'S A WONDERFUL LIFE/VERTIGO
* EDWARD SCISSORHANDS/BREAKFAST CLUB
* PHILADELPHIA/BIG
* APOLLO 13/FRIDAY THE 13TH
* THE COLOR PURPLE/SISTER ACT
* PEE WEE'S BIG ADVENTURE/BATMAN RETURNS
* RISKY BUSINESS/FAR AND AWAY

- ✱ B<small>ILL AND</small> T<small>ED'S</small> E<small>XCELLENT</small> A<small>DVENTURE</small>/M<small>UCH</small> A<small>DO ABOUT</small> N<small>OTHING</small>
- ✱ S<small>ILENCE OF THE</small> L<small>AMBS</small>/F<small>REAKY</small> F<small>RIDAY</small>
- ✱ D<small>ICK</small> T<small>RACY</small>/E<small>VITA</small>
- ✱ H<small>ALLOWEEN</small>/M<small>Y</small> G<small>IRL</small>
- ✱ B<small>ULLITT</small>/T<small>HE</small> B<small>LOB</small>
- ✱ JFK/T<small>HE</small> C<small>OAL</small> M<small>INER'S</small> D<small>AUGHTER</small>
- ✱ T<small>HE</small> P<small>OSIDEON</small> A<small>DVENTURE</small>/A<small>IRPLANE</small>
- ✱ T<small>HE</small> G<small>HOST AND</small> M<small>R.</small> C<small>HICKEN</small>/T<small>HE</small> A<small>PPLE</small> D<small>UMPLING</small> G<small>ANG</small>
- ✱ S<small>LEEPLESS IN</small> S<small>EATTLE</small>/A<small>MITYVILLE</small> 3-D
- ✱ B<small>ARBARELLA</small>/ N<small>INE TO</small> F<small>IVE</small>
- ✱ M<small>ALCOLM</small> X/G<small>LORY</small>
- ✱ S<small>TEEL</small> M<small>AGNOLIAS</small>/T<small>HE</small> P<small>ELICAN</small> B<small>RIEF</small>

Now add your own dynamic duos to this collection.

SMILEAGE

107

No Place Like Home

- ⊛ What's the most unusual item in your closet right now?
- ⊛ What's the most unusual detail or oddity about your home?
- ⊛ What's under your bed?
- ⊛ What smells like home to you?
- ⊛ What's the warmest place in your house?
- ⊛ What's your favorite chair or sofa?
- ⊛ What is your favorite picture that can be seen in your home?
- ⊛ What's your favorite room?
- ⊛ What's your favorite memory that occurred in your home in the past year?
- ⊛ Besides where you live, whose house feels like home to you? Why?

Man the "Or's"

Using whatever criteria seem appropriate, take your pick of these choices.

- Fred or Barney
- Wilma or Betty
- Jay Leno or David Letterman
- Jonny Quest or Hadji
- Greg, Peter, or Bobby
- Marsha, Jan, or Cindy
- Hawkeye or B. J.
- Peter Jennings, Tom Brokaw, or Dan Rather
- Betty or Veronica
- Blair, Tootie, Natalie, or Jo
- Billie Joe, Bobbie Jo, or Betty Jo
- Rush Limbaugh or Howard Stern

Now that you've got the idea, express your preferences with your own groupings.

Situation Ethics

Someone once said that life wasn't intended to be a spectator sport. Every day situations occur and you're forced to make decisions based on your code of ethics, your abilities, and your willingness to become involved. Each of the following scenarios invites you to step inside and talk about how you would respond. Honesty counts.

⊛ You are pushing a shopping cart down a sidewalk headed for your car at a local store. Suddenly you see two security guards chasing a person who is headed toward you. What, if anything, do you do?

⊛ While driving at midday on a highway, you see a woman holding a baby standing beside a car with the hood up. You know that it's twenty miles to the nearest exit. What, if anything, do you do?

⊛ You are riding an elevator from the parking garage to the top floor of a high-rise building. A blind person enters on the first floor. You notice that there is no Braille signage for the buttons. What, if anything, do you do or say?

SMILEAGE

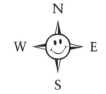

- You make a purchase at a department store and are due five dollars in change. When you get home, you realize that the clerk mistakenly gave you a fifty dollar bill instead. What, if anything, do you do?

- While standing on a sidewalk, you see a truck scrape the fender of an unmanned parked car as it turns a corner. Although it is obvious that the accident has occurred, the truck driver makes no attempt to stop. What, if anything, do you do?

- You are browsing in a small shop when a very pregnant woman slumps to the floor and screams that she's about to have her baby. Including the clerk, there are only two other people besides you in the store. What, if anything, do you do?

- A teenager standing in front of you in line at a busy fast-food restaurant appears to be short in paying for his $4.50 meal. He asks to no one in particular, "Would anyone give me seventy-five cents?" What, if anything, do you do?

- While walking across a mall parking lot, you see a crying baby in a carriage, but no one appears to be caring for the child. What, if anything, do you do?

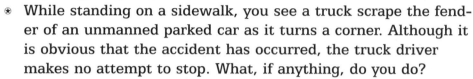

SMILEAGE

N
W · E
S

Family Time

If you're traveling with members of your family, allow these questions to take you back to good old days and maybe evern learn something new.

⊛ Talk your family tree back as many generations as you can— what were the names of the people, where did they live, what were their professions, how many children did they have, what were they most known for?
⊛ What sayings or catchphrases run in your family?
⊛ Who in your family has the best sense of humor? The best laugh? The most cunning mind? Who responds best in a crisis?
⊛ If people aboard have been married, open the floor to tales of courtship.
⊛ What are the five funniest true stories from life in your family?
⊛ What would your family refer to as "hard times"?
⊛ Unless your ancestry is Native American, how long ago did your family come to the United States?
⊛ What heirlooms, such as pieces of furniture, jewelry, quilts, or photographs, are especially significant to your family?
⊛ What recipes have been in your family for years?

Fear-Some Thoughts

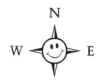

Hodophobia is the fear of travel. If you get flaky at the sight of snow, you're chionophobic. Can't stand the thought of sitting down? That's thaasophobia. Dare to answer the following questions by remembering what President Franklin D. Roosevelt said: "The only thing we have to fear is fear itself."

- What's the scariest movie you've ever seen?
- What's the single most frightening scene in a movie or TV show you've seen?
- Tell about a time when you were really scared by a real-life event.
- What are some things that frighten you?
- Do you have unusual fears, phobias, or worries? Are there situations that raise your anxiety level?
- What's the single greatest act of bravery you've ever witnessed?
- Tell about a time that you faced one of your fears.

SMILEAGE

N
W · E
S

Other Capitals of the World

You know that Washington, D.C., is the capital of the United States. Maybe you even know that Kathmandu is the capital of Nepal. But do you know about these other self-proclaimed capital cities?

* Chocolate Capital of the World—Hershey, Pennsylvania
* Entertainment Capital of the World—Las Vegas, Nevada
* Musky Capital of the World—Boulder Junction, Wisconsin
* Balsam Fir Christmas Tree Capital of the World—Lunenburg County, Nova Scotia
* Onion Capital of the World—Vidalia, Georgia
* Copper Capital of the World—Kearny, Arizona
* Carpet Capital of the World—Dalton, Georgia
* Rattlesnake Capital of the World—Sweetwater, Texas
* Mule Capital of the World—Bishop, California
* Potato Capital of the World—Blackfoot, Idaho
* Poultry Capital of the World—Gainesville, Georgia
* Rose Capital of the World—Tyler, Texas
* Barbecue Capital of the World—Kansas City, Missouri

- Salmon Capitals of the World—Ketchikan, Alaska, and Port Alberni, British Columbia
- Peanut Capital of the World—Dothan, Alabama
- Blueberry Capital of the World—Cherryfield, Maine
- Plow Capital of the World—Moline, Illinois
- Red Flannel Capital of the World—Cedar Springs, Michigan
- Wurst Sausage Capital of the World—Sheboygan, Wisconsin

N

W · E

S

Stinky Pinky

The objective here is to get your friends to guess the pair of rhyming words you have in mind by giving them a definition and the number of syllables in the words. The idea is best communicated in a series of examples.

If the clue is "saltine organizer, Stinky Pinky," you know that the first two words are a way of defining or describing the pair of words. "Stinky" and "Pinky" are two-syllable words, so you know that you're looking for two-syllable words as the answer. The answer here is "cracker packer."

Three-syllable words are pronounced "stah-hin-ky, pah-hin-ky"; four-syllable words are "stah-hink-i-ty, pah-hink-i-ty"; and five-syllable words are "stah-hink-kink-i-ty, pah-hink-kink-i-ty." If you get to six-syllable words, you're on your own.

Here are a few more examples to help you get going:

The Clue	The Syllables	The Answer
grizzly seat	Stink Pink	bear chair
sea movement	Stinky Pinky	ocean motion
evil clergyman	Stah-hin-ky Pah-hin-ky	sinister minister

Stranded Again

Just after dark your car crashes into a ditch during a blinding snowstorm on a lonely mountain road. You will not be found for at least twenty-four hours. You have no food or water supply with you. The temperatures will drop to thirty degrees below zero, and the total snow accumulation will reach three feet. How will you respond to this situation?

N
W E
S

Outrageous Extremes

When trying to give you encouragement, has a friend ever asked, "What's the worst that could happen?" Instead of minimizing the problem, maximize it to Monty Python-esque extremes in these situations.

Example:
Your car horn won't cut off. A taxi driver thinks you're mad at him, so he jumps out of his car to fight, but he can't hear you trying to explain over the horn's blare, so he starts trying to force open your door, so you swerve around him, driving past a hospital where your horn wakes up all the babies, causing more angry people to chase you. In a panicked attempt to get away, you drive your car off a bridge.

⊛ Your belt breaks in a library.
⊛ Your lip gets caught in the zipper of a jacket.
⊛ While in the bathroom, a snake crawls up through the drain.
⊛ The accelerator of your car gets stuck.

- Someone tickles you on a crowded city bus.
- You accidentally take someone else's shopping cart in the grocery store.
- By mistake, you immerse your hand in Super Glue.
- You're riding behind a gang of leather-clad motorcycle riders.
- Because of a nervous tic, you uncontrollably blink in such a way that it looks like a wink.
- An earthquake occurs while you're in a pet shop.
- A bee flies up your skirt or trousers while attending an outdoor wedding.
- During a job interview, your prospective new boss falls asleep, causing his toupee to slide sideways.

N
W E
S

Movie Quotes Potpourri

Can you identify these lines from movies through the years? To diffuse grumbling, none of the films are foreign, obscure, or home-made.

⊛ "You're my best friend, Hoke."
⊛ "Only a penitent man may enter."
⊛ "Does your dog bite?"
⊛ "Ditto."
⊛ "Sorry, folks. The park is closed. The moose at the gate should have told ya."
⊛ "Blaine? His name is Blaine? That's a major appliance. That's not a name."
⊛ "Kickboxing, sport of the future."
⊛ "I wish I had a theater that was only open when it rained."
⊛ "To infinity and beyond!"
⊛ "Too many notes."
⊛ "Don't do it, Miss Celie. He ain't worth it."
⊛ "You put a good burn on the chicken."
⊛ "May the Schwartz be with you."

* "God creates dinosaurs. God destroys dinosaurs. God creates man. Man destroys God. Man creates dinosaurs."
* "I know it's not 1926. I just need it to be."
* "Bring me those puppies!"
* "Give me back my son!"
* "Show me the money!"
* "Prediction? Pain."
* "You're not bad. You're just in pain."
* "I was born a poor black child."

Strange Connections

How good are you at making dissimilar items fit together? Working solo or in teams, include each set of the three items into an imaginative short story or perhaps just a sentence.

- Eskimo, high heels, banana
- King Kong, cotton candy, pogo stick
- lasagna, cowboy, surfboard
- alien spaceship, 8-track tape, piñata
- spurs, curlers, bagpipes
- bank robber, kangaroo, field hockey
- stork, Gummi bears, sumo wrestler
- tango, plumber, ballerina slippers
- waterbed, bottle rockets, Uncle Wally
- kangaroo, breadsticks, tuba
- water balloons, lawn mower, Buckingham Palace
- chain saw, pizza delivery guy, angry bees
- handcuffs, nun, sardines
- strawberry shortcake, dentist, bungee cord
- TV dinner, karate, the cast of the Ice Capades

Explain the Inexplicable

Barbers say that you should never talk about politics or religion. Here are some additional topics that may generate some serious differences of opinion or make food for thought. Be nice.

- Did Lee Harvey Oswald act alone in the assassination of JFK?
- Do you believe in ghosts?
- Could Elvis have faked his death?
- What do you think has caused the disappearance of ships and planes and other strange phenomena in the Bermuda Triangle?
- Do you believe in ESP?
- What is your explanation for the Loch Ness Monster?
- What happened to Jimmy Hoffa?
- Could the moon landing have been faked?
- Could Bigfoot really exist?
- Do you believe in alien beings? If so, do you think they have visited the earth?

Thinking with Thinkers

Below is a cornucopia of quotable quotes from a diverse group of thinkers. Respond to the ideas they pose.

⊛ "I've never met a man I didn't like," Will Rogers said. Who is the most likable person you've ever met? What made that person so enjoyable?

⊛ "You can survive on your own. You can grow on your own. You can even prevail on your own. But you cannot become human on your own," Frederick Buechner said. Do you agree with this statement?

⊛ "Where all men think alike, no one thinks very much," Walter Lippman said. In what areas do you think you hold views that are different from the majority of people?

⊛ "The greatest thing in the world is not so much where we stand as in what direction we're moving," Oliver Wendell Holmes said. In what directions would you say your life is moving? Be as specific as possible.

⊛ "The only cure for suffering is to face it head-on, grab it around the neck, and use it," Mary Craig said. Can you think of any way that you or others you know have been able to make suffering useful?

* "Anything worth doing is worth doing badly," G. K. Chesterton said. What activities do you pursue just because you enjoy them, not because you're good at them?

* "The greatest tragedy of today's convenient world is that you can live a trivial life and get away with it," Tim Hansel wrote. Is it possible to live a trivial life? If so, what is the antidote to this affliction?

* "In the midst of winter I finally discovered within me an invincible summer," Albert Camus said. Is there an invincible summer inside of you? If so, what is the source of its power?

* "Excellence is to do a common thing in an uncommon way," Booker T. Washington said. Are there activities that you pursue in an uncommon way?

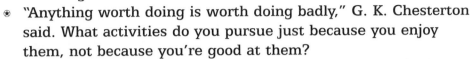

SMILEAGE

Sports Talk

* Who is the greatest coach of all time?
* Describe the most amazing football plays you've ever seen.
* If you were going to put together a dream team for your favorite sport, who would be on it?
* What changes could you make to the following sports to improve them?
    * Baseball
    * Basketball
    * Football
    * Hockey
    * NASCAR racing
    * Soccer

Either/Or Scenarios

Would you rather . . .

* plant a garden or clean your house?
* be a contestant on WHEEL OF FORTUNE or JEOPARDY?
* bathe a hyperactive cocker spaniel or paint a room?
* try to fall asleep with a dripping faucet in your house or loud music coming from next door?
* suffer with laryngitis for three days or have a twenty-four-hour virus?
* watch THE GRINCH WHO STOLE CHRISTMAS or A CHARLIE BROWN CHRISTMAS?
* sustain a broken arm or broken nose?
* become a stand-up comedian or a rodeo clown?
* sit on a plane next to a crying baby or an arguing couple?
* host a talk show or be a guest?
* travel to the world's poverty areas providing help or adopt a needy child?
* die unexpectedly and painlessly at age forty or die at age eighty following an uncomfortable two-year illness?

SMILEAGE

Creative Thinking

- ⊛ Come up with ten things that you have in common with your traveling companions.
- ⊛ You've just been given the opportunity to throw the party of your dreams for twenty-five people with an unlimited expense account. Come up with the what, when, and where for this big event.
- ⊛ Nowhere does creativity run wilder than in the naming of beauty parlors and barbershops. From coast to coast, you'll find names like Mane Attraction, Head Hunters, and A Kut Above. What name would you give your hair salon?
- ⊛ It's your job to come up with a site for the Grand Masters Tournament of Hide-and-Seek. Where should it be played?
- ⊛ What feature would you add to an automobile that is not currently available?
- ⊛ Which sports should be added to the Olympics? Which should be removed?
- ⊛ If Elvis were alive today, where would he be?
- ⊛ According to legend, Daniel Boone carved "D. Boon kilt a bar" in a tree to memorialize his accomplishment. If you were going to

create a landmark for one of your personal achievements, where would it be, what sort of monument would you create, and what would it say?

❋ In the movie MISS FIRECRACKER, Tim Robbins plays a man who picks up roadkill. What jobs can you think of that would be worse than dead animal removal?

❋ There's a knock at your door. Who do you hope is not there?

❋ No one would want an apartment above a bowling alley. What are some equally unappealing locations?

Initial Responses—The P.S.

Earlier in the book, you were challenged to identify authors by their works. All of the famous (and semifamous) people described below use their initials instead of their given names. Can you identify them?

* contemporary poet known for using lowercase letters
* famous showman quoted as saying, "There's a sucker born every minute"
* infamous character on TV's DALLAS
* legendary bluesman known for hot licks on his guitar named Lucille
* multievent race car driver noted for winning the Indy 500 in '61, '64, '67, and '77
* prominent rapper who declares that ladies love cool James
* law-and-order series that starred William Shatner as the title character
* avant-garde Canadian songstress who debuted with a band called The Re-Clines
* singer who had a 1973 hit with "My Maria"

SMILEAGE

- series that starred Greg Evigan as a trucker whose copilot was a chimpanzee
- two-hit wonder who recorded the CB radio recitation "Convoy"
- Harvard psychologist who supported his theory of trained learning by placing animals in a specially designed box
- country-pop vocalist whose signature song is "Raindrops Keep Fallin' On My Head"
- 1975 movie starring Burt Reynolds as the manager of an up-and-coming country band

In Your Opinion

If you can't express your convictions without being gracious, skip this page. If you can, generate some stimulating conversations with these questions.

⊛ If you could change one law in this country, what would it be?
⊛ Who is the most powerful person in the world?
⊛ Many people have expressed their solutions to the world's drug problem, including more education, more resources for rehabilitation, and decriminalization of drugs. What would you propose?
⊛ The prison system has skyrocketed in the past decade so that it has become an enormous economic burden on cities, counties, states, and the federal government. What practical steps should be taken to solve this problem?
⊛ Almost everyone agrees that the welfare system needs reform. What would you say are the first steps that should be taken?
⊛ Is capital punishment morally wrong?
⊛ Should animal testing be allowed for medical research?

Silly Syllables

Sing the song "Row, Row, Row Your Boat" with each person singing only one syllable. For example, one person will sing "gen-", the next sings "-tly", the next "down", the next "the," etc. You work around a circle. Whoever messes up is out, so you start again from the top. If you survive this song, try another.

Jingle Jangle

Do these timeless slogans and jingle lyrics remind you of the products they promoted?

- ✹ "The real thing"
- ✹ "Two-all-beef-patties-special-sauce-lettuce-cheese-pickles-onions-on-a-sesame-seed bun"
- ✹ "You'll wonder where the yellow went when you brush your teeth with _____"
- ✹ "See the U.S.A. in a _____"
- ✹ "Quality Is Job One"
- ✹ "My bologna has a first name. It's _-_-_-_-_."
- ✹ "The dogs kids love to bite"
- ✹ "Choosy mothers choose _____"
- ✹ "We love to fly and it shows"
- ✹ "We're Number Two. We have to try harder."
- ✹ "Everything is better when it sits on a _____"
- ✹ "We're looking for a few good men"
- ✹ "Have it your way"
- ✹ "The Un-cola"
- ✹ "Just do it"

The Lost Art of Giving Directions

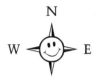

"You can't get there from here"—at least not by following the directions most people give. Northerners sound so confident that they must know what they're talking about, and southerners seem so friendly that you want to trust them.

Add to this collection of phrases that will get you nowhere fast.

- ❋ "When you see the intersection, don't turn there."
- ❋ "If you cross the bridge, you've gone too far."
- ❋ "Turn just past where the barn used to be."
- ❋ "Go up this road a-ways."
- ❋ "Just keep going."

SMILEAGE

Who Am I?

See how many clues you need to identify the following well-known people.

1. I was born in Temun, Russia, in 1888 and immigrated to New York City in 1892.
2. My first job in music was working at a Bowery cafe as a singing waiter.
3. I taught myself to play piano, but only in the key of F-sharp, and I never learned musical notation.
4. The first inductee into the Songwriter's Hall of Fame, I am considered one of the most successful and prolific songwriters of all time.
5. My repertoire includes "God Bless America," "There's No Business Like Show Business," "Blue Skies," "Easter Parade," and "White Christmas."

1. I was born on Christmas Day 1642 in Woolsthorpe, England.
2. Curious about all things mechanical, as a boy I built a mill powered by a mouse.
3. In 1669 I became a mathematics professor at Cambridge University and am credited with inventing integral and differential calculus.

SMILEAGE

136

4. I constructed a reflecting telescope and unlocked many mysteries involving light and color.
5. I was the first person to state the laws of gravitation.

1. I was born the fourth of twelve children in my parents' Tennessee mountain home.
2. After finding some success in music in Knoxville, I moved to Nashville in 1964.
3. Among my hit songs are "Jolene," "I Will Always Love You," and "Love Is Like a Butterfly."
4. I starred in popular movies including NINE TO FIVE and STEEL MAGNOLIAS.
5. I'm famous for my wigs, my outrageous outfits, and my even-more-outrageous figure.

1. I was born in the slums of New Orleans in 1900.
2. As a boy, I was sent to a reform school where I learned to play cornet.
3. By 1929, I was the most widely known black musician in the world.
4. I earned the nickname "Satchmo" because people said I had a satchel mouth.
5. Among my most popular songs are "What a Wonderful World," "Hello, Dolly," "Mame," and "Mack the Knife."

SMILEAGE

N
W • E
S

Spellbound

The game here is to avoid completing the spelling of a word while setting other people up to be forced into spelling one. All words must be at least three letters so you can't lose for spelling words like he, to, or be.

Here's how it is played: The first person offers a letter. The second player then adds a letter. When each person has had the chance to contribute, you continue with the first person. The objective is to know a word that could be spelled but avoid adding a letter that would complete it.

For example:

The first person might say "B" thinking of the word BEAR.

The second person might add an "O" thinking of the word BORE.

The third person might add a "T" thinking of the word BOTH.

The fourth person might add another "T" thinking of the word BOTTLE.

The fifth person might realize how to set up the next person and add the "L" for BOTTLE.

The sixth person might realize a way out by adding an "I" to make the word shift toward BOTTLING.

The seventh person would add the "N" and the eighth person would be forced to finish the word with the "G."

You must know a word that can be completed with the letter you add. In other words, if it's your turn and the letters so far are "T" and "O," you can't add a "Z" because there is not a word with that spelling in the English language.

Powers of Observation

❀ List everything that appears on a penny, a nickel, a dime, a quarter, a dollar bill.

❀ Can you name everything that's in your wallet?

❀ Reconstruct your day so far with as much detail as possible.

❀ Describe the last stranger with whom you exchanged words (a cash register clerk, someone at a rest stop) as accurately as you can.

❀ Pass through any small town and you'll find shops that feature "Video Rentals and Tanning Beds," an unlikely combination. In Louisiana I discovered a store that boasted videos, tanning beds, boots, and fireworks. In Tennessee you'll find one-stop shopping for shoes and cheese and a store that offers scrap metal and herbs. Do you know of stores that offer strange combinations of merchandise?

❀ Inventory the items in the largest drawer in your kitchen.

❀ Pretend everything in your living room has been removed. Your belongings will only be returned if you ask for them specifically. Taking a mental tour, see how many items you can recall.

❋ Sometimes retailers create unintentional humor with their signage. The misspelling of a key word on a sign intended to attract tourists who rode the trolley past one store resulted in "We love trolly people." A convenience store advertising two of its products put the words too close together, which created the highly combustible delicacy "Diesel Fried Chicken." A billboard on a lonely highway meant to inform tourists they could buy produce and old memorabilia, but what it said was "Fruit Antiques." Have you seen signs that inadvertently communicated more than intended?

N
W ⊕ E
S

The Word for Today

If you like puns, this word game is for you. Playing is simple. Just come up with a word that conforms to the patterns shown here:

Examples:

⊛ The word for today is fascinate. F-A-S-C-I-N-A-T-E. I will now attempt to use it in a sentence. My sweater has nine buttons, but I can only fascinate.

⊛ The word for today is pasteurize. P-A-S-T-E-U-R-I-Z-E. I will now attempt to use it in a sentence. When I pitch the ball real hard, it will fly right pasteurize.

⊛ The word for today is Alaska. A-L-A-S-K-A. I will now attempt to use it in a sentence. I don't know if she wants to go out with me, but alaska.

⊛ The word for today is avenue. A-V-E-N-U-E. I will now attempt to use it in a sentence. Avenue bicycle, but my mom won't let me ride it on the street.

⊛ The word for today is distress. D-I-S-T-R-E-S-S. I will now attempt to use it in a sentence. I don't think distress fits me like it used to.

Missing Lyrics

If your fellow travelers are musically inclined, make things a little trickier by modifying these songs as follows:

⊛ Sing "You Are My Sunshine" leaving out the pronouns.
⊛ Try leaving out the articles "a," "an," and "the" while singing "Pop Goes the Weasel," "Bingo," or "Jingle Bells."

Now you've got the idea, add your own challenges.

Where Would You Be If . . . ?

If you were experiencing the following, identify the state where you would be.

* Getting soaked by the mist rising from Niagara Falls.
* Coming face-to-face with Mount Rushmore.
* Basking in the sun beneath the southernmost latitude in the continental U.S.
* Hiking up Pike's Peak.
* Taking a picture of Diamond Head.
* Staring up at the Gateway to the West.
* Attending a game at Mile High Stadium.
* Descending into Carlsbad Caverns.
* Look above the clouds to see the summit of Mount McKinley.
* Studying the crack on the Liberty Bell.
* Reenacting the Wright Brothers' flight at Kitty Hawk.
* Standing near Plymouth Rock.
* Cheering in the Hoosierdome.

Tongue Twisters

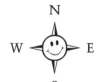

Take a turn at tackling these wacky word combinations. Say each three or five times—if you can.

* Rubber baby buggy bumpers
* Warren ran with record reruns.
* Spock's stock is shock schlock.
* Blake Brock broke a bleak black block.
* Must have missed her master's mister.
* Clean the clips, clocks, cots, and kettles.
* A big, black bug bit a big, black bear, made the big, black bear bleed blood.
* Fat frogs flying past fast
* Lesser leather never weathered wetter weather better.
* Smother Smith's Fish Sauce Shop
* Knapsack straps
* Greek grapes

N
W · E
S

Whiz Quiz

"When you've gotta go, you've gotta go," goes the old saying. But that doesn't mean bathroom stops won't start conflicts. Courtesy of urologist Dr. Jerry Conway, test your knowledge relating to the call of nature.

A man needs to make a bathroom visit less frequently than a woman because:

a. His bladder size is typically 20 percent larger than a woman's.

b. His bladder walls are thinner, allowing for greater expansion.

c. It is a myth with no significant anatomical basis.

Approximately how much urine can the healthy adult bladder hold?

a. 100-200 cc

b. 250-300 cc

c. 400-500 cc

Which of the following drinks will run through your system the fastest?

    a. hot chocolate

    b. water

    c. Diet Coke

How many minutes after it is consumed is a glass of water ready to make an exit?

    a. 10-15 minutes

    b. 20-30 minutes

    c. 45-60 minutes

True or false:

    It is good to have a full bladder in the event of a car wreck because the liquid will absorb the shock.

Final Topics of Conversation

- ✹ In your opinion, what is the strangest-looking animal?
- ✹ What's the most architecturally striking building you've ever seen?
- ✹ When you think about being on a beach, where do you see yourself?
- ✹ What is the worst experience you've had in a restaurant?
- ✹ What are your favorite Far Side cartoons?
- ✹ What's the best bread you've ever eaten?
- ✹ List three fragrances or smells that you find appealing.
- ✹ What's the darkest place you've ever been?
- ✹ Describe a time when you felt really miserable.
- ✹ What's a question you would like to ask God?
- ✹ What's something significant you feel that you've learned in the past year?

Answers

With a Little Help from Their Friends, PAGE 15
- Dawn
- the Vandellas
- the Heartbreakers
- the Comets
- the Union Gap
- the Blackhearts
- the Shondells
- the Gang
- Miami Sound Machine
- Tenille
- the Family Stone
- the Miracles
- the Royal Canadians
- the New Bohemians
- the Sunshine Band
- the Pips

State Nicknames, PAGE 18
- Tennessee
- New Jersey
- Vermont
- Nebraska
- Missouri
- Minnesota
- Alaska
- Illinois
- Louisiana
- Massachusetts
- Washington
- Texas
- Virginia
- Nevada

Quotable Movies: The Classics, PAGE 20
- IT'S A WONDERFUL LIFE
- DRACULA
- GONE WITH THE WIND
- THE MALTESE FALCON
- CASABLANCA
- CITIZEN KANE

- Yankee Doodle Dandy
- On the Waterfront
- The Grapes of Wrath
- To Kill a Mockingbird
- Harvey
- All About Eve
- Monkey Business
- My Little Chickadee
- Grand Hotel
- Bringing Up Baby
- Duck Soup
- A Night at the Opera
- The Wizard of Oz

Who Am I?, PAGE 22
- Charlie Chaplin
- Ludwig von Beethoven
- Amelia Earhart
- Christopher Columbus

TV Trivia, PAGE 24
- Arnold's
- Ponderosa
- Endora
- The Honeymooners

- Rawhide
- Steve McGarrett
- St. Eligius
- Family Ties
- General Lee
- Nuclear power plant
- You'll Never Get Rich and Sgt. Bilko
- Lilith
- Cement pond
- The one-armed man
- As the Stomach Turns
- Allen Ludden
- The Cosby Show
- Dan Rowan and Dick Martin
- Daniel Boone
- Eight Is Enough
- Walnut Grove
- Agent 99
- Walter Cronkite
- Lurch

Animal Riddles, PAGE 26
- in his trunk
- He doesn't like to stick his neck out.

- cubcakes
- Pupsicles
- Chilly dogs
- Coca-Koala
- by the peck
- There are quackers in their bed.
- hare remover
- a fang-you note

The Big Quiz, PAGE 29
- The Big Easy
- Big Bird
- Big Mac
- Big Sky Country
- Big Brother
- The Big Valley
- Big Jake
- The Big Bopper
- Big Bang Theory
- Big Apple
- Big Top
- Big Ben
- Big Bertha
- Bigfoot

Quotable Movies: The '60s, PAGE 31
- THE SOUND OF MUSIC
- PSYCHO
- MARY POPPINS
- TRUE GRIT
- WEST SIDE STORY
- HELLO, DOLLY
- EASY RIDER
- DR. STRANGELOVE: OR, HOW I LEARNED TO STOP WORRYING AND LOVE THE BOMB
- 2001: A SPACE ODYSSEY

Spinoffs, PAGE 41
- THE MARY TYLER MOORE SHOW
- THE MARY TYLER MOORE SHOW
- THE MARY TYLER MOORE SHOW
- CHEERS
- HAPPY DAYS
- HAPPY DAYS
- M*A*S*H*
- DIFF'RENT STROKES
- DALLAS
- THE CAVALCADE OF STARS

N
W ← → E
S

SMILEAGE

SMILEAGE

Quotable Movies: The '70s, PAGE 55

- MONTY PYTHON AND THE HOLY GRAIL
- STAR WARS
- BLAZING SADDLES
- YOUNG FRANKENSTEIN
- DIRTY HARRY
- AMERICAN GRAFFITI
- BUTCH CASSIDY AND THE SUNDANCE KID
- THE GODFATHER
- LOVE STORY
- DIRTY HARRY
- TAXI DRIVER
- ANNIE HALL
- ROCKY

Geography Quiz, PAGE 56

- California, Arizona, New Mexico, Texas
- Maine, Maryland, Massachusetts, Michigan, Minnesota, Mississippi, Missouri, Montana
- Washington, Oregon, California, Alaska, Oregon
- Florida, Alabama, Mississippi, Louisiana, Texas
- Virginia
- Atlanta, Georgia; Augusta, Maine; Annapolis, Maryland; Albany, New York; Austin, Texas
- Lake of the Woods, Minnesota
- Missouri, Kentucky, Arkansas, Tennessee, Mississippi, Louisiana, Minnesota, Wisconsin, Iowa, Illinois
- California
- Arizona
- Little Rock, Arkansas; Des Moines, Iowa; Baton Rouge, Louisiana; St. Paul, Minnesota; Jefferson City, Missouri; Carson City, Nevada; Santa Fe, New Mexico; Oklahoma City, Oklahoma
- Alabama, Arkansas, Georgia, Kentucky, Mississippi, Missouri, North Carolina, Virginia
- Alaska

N

W — E

S

SMILEAGE

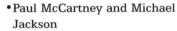

Initial Responses, PAGE 60
- H. G. Wells
- J. R. R. Tolkien
- E. B. White
- J. D. Salinger
- R. L. Stine
- S. E. Hinton
- T. S. Eliot
- C. S. Lewis
- A. A. Milne

Just Duet, PAGE 64
- Flatt & Scruggs
- Elton John and Kiki Dee
- Simon and Garfunkel
- Celine Dion and Peabo Bryson
- Bill Medley and Jennifer Warnes
- Dionne Warwick and the Spinners
- Run DMC and Aerosmith
- Marilyn McCoo and Billy Davis, Jr.
- Patti LaBelle and Michael McDonald
- Paul McCartney and Stevie Wonder
- Paul McCartney and Michael Jackson
- Natalie Cole and Nat King Cole
- Sonny and Cher
- Kenny Rogers and Dolly Parton
- Peter Cetera and Amy Grant
- Neil Diamond and Barbra Streisand
- Joe Cocker and Jennifer Warnes
- Diana Ross and Lionel Richie
- Olivia Newton-John and John Travolta
- James Ingram and Michael McDonald
- Nancy Sinatra and Frank Sinatra
- Marvin Gaye and Tammi Terrell
- Kenny Rogers and Kim Carnes
- Conway Twitty and Loretta Lynn
- Johnny Mathis and Deniece Williams
- James Ingram and Linda Ronstadt
- k.d. lang and Roy Orbison
- George Jones and Tammy Wynette
- Diana Ross and the Supremes and the Temptations

The Little Quiz, PAGE 66

- LITTLE HOUSE ON THE PRAIRIE
- Little Big Horn
- LITTLE WOMEN
- Little Rock
- THE LITTLE PRINCESS
- LITTLE LORD FAUNTLEROY
- "Little Deuce Coupe"
- LITTLE SHOP OF HORRORS
- Li'l Abner
- Little John
- "A Little Bit of Soap"
- Little Dipper
- Little League
- Little Richard
- Little Rascals
- Little Orphan Annie
- LITTLE MISS MARKER
- THE LITTLE MERMAID
- Little Red Riding Hood

Where in the World Would You Be . . . ?, PAGE 71

- China
- Egypt
- Nepal or Tibet
- Spain
- New Zealand
- Australia
- Zimbabwee
- Italy
- Germany
- Japan
- Norway
- India
- Kenya

It's a Tree but Not a Bush, PAGE 73

The secret here is that one word has double letters; the other does not. Both have something in common which generally throws people for a loop. Here are some more examples to offer:

- It's Goodyear but not Firestone.
- It's Arnold Schwarzenegger but not Mel Gibson.

If you want to add a torture factor, act as though it is really difficult to come up with pairs. When people offer you their guesses, appear to be going through a complex evaluation to determine if they have a correct answer.

Sports Alias, PAGE 75
- Wilt Chamberlain
- William Perry
- Ed Jones
- Pete Maravich
- Jack Nicklaus
- Lou Gerhig
- Joe Greene
- Joe DiMaggio
- Joe Frazier
- Joe Jackson
- Joe Namath
- Florence Griffith-Joyner
- Stan Musial
- Reggie White
- Don Meredith
- Lamar Lundy, Deacon Jones, Rosey Grier, Merlin Olsen

Great Beginnings in Literature, PAGE 80
- A TALE OF TWO CITIES
- MOBY DICK
- THE HUNCHBACK OF NOTRE DAME
- DAVID COPPERFIELD
- THE ADVENTURES OF TOM SAWYER
- 1984
- FRANKENSTEIN
- TREASURE ISLAND
- ROMEO AND JULIET
- LES MISERABLES
- OF MICE AND MEN
- THE DIARY OF ANNE FRANK
- THE CATCHER IN THE RYE

Quotable Movies: The '80s, PAGE 82
- THE TERMINATOR
- TOP GUN
- THE BREAKFAST CLUB
- RAISING ARIZONA
- THE PRINCESS BRIDE
- THE BLUES BROTHERS
- FIELD OF DREAMS

SMILEAGE

N

W E

S

Lasagne, Puzzler, Colonel Gumm, Dr. Cassandra, Clock King, Marsha, Esmeralda, and Minstrel

Two Clues, One Answer, PAGE 92
- Pluto
- Topaz
- Casablanca
- Platoon
- Apollo
- Independence Day
- blackjack

Science Test, PAGE 95
- Pluto, Neptune, Uranus, Saturn, Jupiter, Mars, Earth, Venus, Mercury
- centrifugal force
- 0 degrees
- Petri dish
- carnivore
- troposphere
- electron
- sulphur

- recessive
- photosynthesis

By Any Other Name, PAGE 98
- Mark Twain
- Superman
- Marilyn Monroe
- Dr. Seuss
- Vanilla Ice
- The Shadow
- Nicholas Cage
- Judy Garland
- Rock Hudson
- Sting
- Whoopi Goldberg
- Batman
- John Wayne
- Cher

Quotable Movies: The '90s, PAGE 100
- A FEW GOOD MEN
- WAYNE'S WORLD
- MISERY

SMILEAGE

- DEAD POETS SOCIETY
- SILENCE OF THE LAMBS
- DANCES WITH WOLVES
- APOLLO 13
- THE FUGITIVE
- THE LION KING
- HOOK
- THE USUAL SUSPECTS
- SCHINDLER'S LIST
- CITY SLICKERS

Literal Translations, PAGE 101

- have the body
- according to the menu
- out of many, one
- in juice
- after the fashion
- always faithful
- joy of living
- such is life
- what will be, will be
- black film
- outside of the main course
- until I see you again
- for (the) good
- we came, we saw, we conquered

Role Reversals, PAGE 106

- Harrison Ford
- Robert Duvall
- Dustin Hoffman
- Richard Dreyfuss
- Susan Sarandon
- O. J. Simpson
- Dan Ackroyd
- Robert Redford
- Jimmy Stewart
- Anthony Michael Hall
- Tom Hanks
- Kevin Bacon
- Whoopi Goldberg
- Paul Reubens
- Tom Cruise
- Keanu Reeves
- Jody Foster
- Madonna
- Jamie Lee Curtis
- Steve McQueen
- Sissy Spacek
- Leslie Nielsen
- Don Knotts
- Meg Ryan
- Jane Fonda

SMILEAGE

SMILEAGE

- Jif
- Delta
- Avis
- Ritz
- Marines
- Burger King
- 7-Up
- Nike

Who Am I, PAGE 136
- Irving Berlin
- Isaac Newton
- Dolly Parton
- Louis Armstrong

Where Would You Be If . . . ?,
PAGE 144
- New York
- South Dakota
- Florida
- Colorado
- Hawaii
- Missouri
- Colorado

- New Mexico
- Alaska
- Pennsylvania
- North Carolina
- Massachusetts
- Indiana

Whiz Quiz, PAGE 146
- c. It is a myth because the bladder's capacity for men and women is approximately the same.
- c.
- c.
- b.
- False. A full bladder may burst upward, causing damage to the abdomen.

ISBN 1-888952-43-1

6 10529 00039 1